Sport & motivation

INSPIRING STORIES
FOR SYNCING MIND, BODY & SPIRIT

PETE MOORE *with* **RENEE BROWN**

Mercury Press, Rochester, New York

CONTENTS

No one who achieves success does so
without acknowledging the help of others.
The wise and confident acknowledge this help
with gratitude.
— ALFRED NORTH WHITEHEAD,
ENGLISH MATHEMATICIAN AND PHILOSOPHER

I KNEW THREE THINGS as a young child growing up in the Florida panhandle: swimming in the ocean, going to church and fishing with my grandmother. And, I knew I was loved.

I also knew at a very early age there were rules in our house that I needed to follow. My parents' rules were statements, not questions. My dad used to tell me if I acted up I would be in deep trouble. He was old-school military, a confident man who commanded respect. We lived on Tyndall Air Force Base, 12 miles east of Panama City, where he was stationed. If asked, my mom and dad would say I was never a problem and I didn't act up in school because I knew better. Well, I never really wanted to find out what deep trouble actually involved, so they were correct, I did know better. My parents gave tough love, but it was unconditional love.

Each day after school I could play until five o'clock and then I had to go inside and do my homework. I also had to read and do other studies that weren't homework assignments, but literally home-assigned studies, until it was time to go to bed. I remember thinking how unfair it was to make me come inside, sit at the table until I'd eaten all of my dinner, and then retreat to my desk where I would study until it was time to go to bed. I wanted to be outside playing with my friends, but I never expressed that frustration. I knew better. My dad would say it was character molding: If I were to become a leader, I needed to set a good example.

During the hours I was allowed to play outside I always seemed to be the play magnet, the kid everyone wanted to be around. My mother used to call me the Pied Piper of the neighborhood—it didn't matter what I was doing, there was always a trail of kids behind me. In hindsight it's easy for me to recognize the lessons my parents were teaching me at the time. My dad had recognized something—I became a leader at an early age.

> *You find yourself living the old cliché:*
> *I'm now my parents. But that is a compliment.*

Living in the Florida panhandle, so near the ocean, we would frequently go swimming in the Gulf of Mexico. We also went with my grandmother to the coasts of Mississippi and Alabama to fish and swim. She would gather up a carload of kids that included my cousins and several foster children she took care of, and head out. If my uncle was along, he and I would net fish off the Pensacola Bridge. We would set crab traps and spend hours on the water. I was content and happy. My grandmother and mother were both magnificent in the kitchen and used the fish we caught on our day trip to prepare what I considered the best catfish, shrimp and grits platters this side of the Mississippi. Sitting at my grandmother's dinner table, rehashing our day's excursions, is a video I often replay in my mind. The smell of catfish, shrimp and grits, though rare now, as I live in the northeast, still stops me in my tracks.

Paul, a colleague of my dad's, regularly stopped by our house for a visit. He understood my family and the beliefs that underlay our life's journey.

He would sit down and I would quietly listen as he read the bible to me. I remember being at peace as he read, a calm that was inexplicable at my young age. I didn't realize at the time that these experiences were all a part of the foundation for my life today.

While I was still young, my grandma took control of my spiritual development. I didn't just go to a one-hour church service every Sunday; I spent a good part of the entire day in church every Sunday. There were no exceptions and no excuses. We would all meet at my Aunt Josephine's house and walk to church together. My Aunt Josephine, like my grandmother, was a very orderly, no-nonsense kind of person. I learned at an early age to address all adults with "Yes, ma'am," or "Yes, sir," replies I still voice as a grownup. Did I ever miss church? Not a chance.

Our place of worship was Trinity Baptist Church in Pensacola, Florida. I began my day with Sunday school, and then transitioned to bible study class, followed by a church service in the sanctuary that lasted several hours. For a young boy those few hours seemed like several days but I never complained to my aunt or grandmother. I knew better. After the service, the congregation would gather in the fellowship hall and share a meal. There was always a large variety of food but my favorites were southern fried chicken and macaroni and cheese. The church was a place of spiritual consolation—but as a young boy I just remember loving the food.

My grandmother passed away when I was an adult. I attended her funeral at that same Trinity Baptist Church in Pensacola, Florida. Many of the same people were there and much of the same food was served following her burial. My grandmother would have smiled.

I attended one other service at that church before I left for home. The preacher asked, as was his routine, for anyone that wanted to, to stand and proclaim his or her trepidations to the congregation for prayer. For the first time in my life, I stood up. It felt like my grandmother was yanking me out of my seat from above as I tried to sit back down, but couldn't. The preacher asked what my concern was and, though hesitant to begin speaking, I started to share my concerns and apprehensions surrounding a professional decision. The preacher's response was one I will never forget. He told me to get out of the boat and trust that you can tread water. And then we all prayed. I took that chance and have never looked back. My life remains in God's hands. It is a joy to know God.

> *There are no real coincidences in life for those with faith strong enough to recognize coincidences for what they really are: intricate pieces of the providential design God created for each of our lives.*
> —DELIA PARR, AUTHOR

In reflection, I can honestly say I wouldn't be who I am today if it weren't for my grandparents. I was around them all of the time. My grandmother used to tell me to do it the right way. For her *it* was life. Do life the right way. She was the personification of what would become my moral fiber.

> *The true measure of character is the way you act when no one is watching.*

While I was still in elementary school, Dad was transferred from Florida to Hancock Air Force Base, near Syracuse, New York. I left Trinity Baptist, but the spiritual lessons stuck with me. After reading from the bible all those years, the words of the gospel were forming my mind. The messages of the gospel were developing into the way I choose to conduct my life.

> *My life has been scripted out by God and it is God who looks over me.*

I finished community college, married the love of my life and settled in the same suburb of Syracuse my parents had moved to when my dad was transferred. Truthfully, I stopped attending church for a period of time as I got wrapped up in the rush of beginning a new phase of adulthood. Regardless, I remained spiritual. I became more involved with coaching and the seed was planted, sprouting the roots of my lifelong passion. My past is the philosophical foundation I use for the development of young athletes.

As my wife and I prepared for the birth of our son, we started to attend St. Rose of Lima Church, where we still worship. Around this same time I also decided to grow dread locks. It was who I wanted to be. Initially my dad was not very receptive to the look and questioned whether I might be experiencing an identity crisis of some kind. Eventually he accepted my new appearance and I kept the style for eleven years. During this time my reputation as a coach and athletic trainer was growing, as was my philosophy behind the importance of syncing a young athlete's mind, body and spirit. As my reputation grew, friends and colleagues expressed concern that my dread locks were not professional looking and, though I was a great coach, I might not be taken seriously. My wife said the tresses needed to be cut as she was tired of them. So for both professional and personal reasons, I cut the locks. My appearance took a fairly dramatic turn from wearing a Rasta hat encasing thick long dread locks to a buzz cut. It was noticeable, to say the least. Once they were gone many other people commented on how much they missed them and that my locks were a representation of who I was. Had I sold out to the pressure to conform? Was I not practicing what I preach to my athletes? The truth is I'm not a corporate kind of guy and that's not my God-given role or God's plan for me. I'm okay with that—the locks are coming back.

> *Accept me for who I am.*
> *Don't be afraid to be different.*

There are those who don't understand my approach to syncing the mind, body and spirit, but results speak for themselves. Beyond developing good athletes, it develops young kids into respectable and accountable young adults who understand the importance of an education and are positive contributors to their community. It develops kids who respect their parents, put family first, do not use foul language and understand that their athletic prowess is not based on the type of sneaker they put on or the jersey they wear. It's not about the stud kid, it's about every kid. As a trainer and coach, the real success is taking a child with no real talent, no coordination, and no belief in who they are, and turning them into a successful athlete and productive member of society.

I am always on the go, a habit I developed early. My father used to say "Get up early in the morning and go until you fall." My mother's well-known mantra, to this day, is "You get to rest when you're in your grave." She would tell me, "Until then, you need to work, live every minute, and at the end of the day know you have achieved everything you could have —physically, mentally and emotionally." End your day with no doubts so that if something happens tomorrow that leaves you unable to give, you will have no regrets.

From those thoughts come my motivation and resolve in day-to-day living: To live in a manner that is true to God, to be a good role model—particularly to adolescents and young adults—and to bring a faithful presence to youth sports, inspiring young athletes to sync their mind, body and spirit so that they, too, can experience the ultimate in success. The chapters in this book are stories from some of the athletes I've trained over the years. I hope when you are through reading you have the tools you need to become the best coach, the best athlete, and the best person you can be.

I believe

WHEN YOU LOOK AT A PERSON you can learn a lot. My mother used to say "Watch and listen," which is often what I do when I am in places or at events that involve large groups of people. It's fascinating to me to observe a person's aura. It's an impression of who that person is or who they are trying to be. If you watch a person long enough you can begin to determine whether they're a thinker or a show-off, caring or arrogant, a wise guy or withdrawn, all of the above or none of the above. A person's posture and stance, mannerisms, disposition, temperament and mood all tell a story. My mother was so right. I believe you can learn so much through simple observation—watching and listening to other people.

The first thing I do with a young athlete is sit down and have a conversation with them. A part of the conversation may be their interest in a particular sport or a position they wish to play, but my greatest interest is to know who they are as a person. I will learn weaknesses, strengths, attitude and temperament—what it will take to inspire this young person on the journey that will sync their mind, body and spirit. What I glean from these conversations guides me in helping them become the best person they can be, not just the best athlete.

> *My coach gave me the greatest gift anyone*
> *can give. He believed in me.*
> —HOWARD TWILLEY, FOOTBALL HALL OF FAMER

Google the words *mind, body* and *spirit* and you're likely to come across definitions from Merriam-Webster, *Wikipedia*, Oxford Dictionaries and the like with similar descriptions:

MIND —the element of a person that enables them to be aware of the world and their experiences, to think, and to feel; the faculty of consciousness and thought. Synonyms include: intellect, brainpower, understanding, reasoning and judgment.

BODY —the physical structure of a person or an animal, including the bones, flesh, and organs. Synonyms include: figure, frame, form, physique, anatomy and skeleton.

SPIRIT —The nonphysical part of a person that is the seat of emotions and character; the soul. Synonyms include: attitudes, beliefs, principles, standards and ethics.

I work with aspiring young athletes seeking to develop this trinity of sorts—a training trifecta. Striving to bring these three elements into harmony is marked with milestones reached along the way. It takes years to reach fruition. It is about seeking long-term results.

> *Four things for success:*
> *work and pray, think and believe.*
> —NORMAN VINCENT PEALE,
> THE POWER OF POSITIVE THINKING

All kids are coachable, if you truly believe all kids are coachable. I choose not to make a judgment based on what may be a bad first impression, or, reciprocally, to turn a blind eye to poor character because a player shows a certain level of athletic potential. Young talent does not always equate to future potential just as negative behavior does not always mean one will forever be a bad kid.

Young people can be influenced so easily. I continually ask myself, what will make this particular individual a good person as well as a good athlete? What can I do to inspire this young athlete to believe in themselves and to believe in what they are doing? How can I help them discover who they are and where they want to be. What will it take for them to make that transition from backyard game play to competition on a major playing field with other elite athletes?

> *Ability is what you're capable of doing.*
> *Motivation determines what you do.*
> *Attitude determines how well you do it.*
> —LOU HOLTZ, FOOTBALL PLAYER, COACH,
> SPORTSCASTER & MOTIVATIONAL SPEAKER

Jim Forbis, a business executive and motivational speaker, speaks of the mind and spirit as they relate to attitude. His recommendation is to control your attitude, as attitude will navigate success. Forbis makes the statement: "Attitude determines the results of the journey before it begins. A negative thought is a down payment for failure." He goes on to say:

"Look to where you are going, not where you have been. The Lord gave us free will. It is our choice how we handle it," which is true. But more often than not, young impressionable teens need direction to assure the free will they have been blessed with will be handled positively— disciplined and void of negative thoughts and actions.

Wearing A Kobe Bryant T-shirt
Doesn't Make You Kobe Bryant
—UNKNOWN

Motivational speaker Max Moyo, Founder and CEO of Ignite My Potential, believes that imitation leads to limitation. If you are trying to be someone else, you are not being authentic. Moyo perceives each of the seven billion plus people on this planet as unique. He actually refers to each one of us as the eighth wonder of the world, affirming there will never be anyone like us again. Yet people often spend their entire lives trying to be someone else. And, he says, "People suck at trying to be someone else."

Moyo gives this example: "If a fish spends his life trying to learn how to climb a tree, the fish will always feel like a failure. It's about discovering that which you were born to do."

Helping a young person identify their personal goals and aspirations will help guide them to a purpose—*their* purpose. Rick Warren, author of the best-selling book, *The Purpose Driven Life*, writes: "Purpose always produces passion. Nothing energizes like a clear purpose."

Working with young athletes involves inspiration, and commitment and a long-term plan. This transformation is not a quick fix, it is a developmental progression. It's a sequence of actions and behaviors that involve time, maturity and hard work.

My father taught me as a young man to always understand my surroundings. Continually ask yourself what you are doing and why. He refers to it as the *Circle of Why*.

Remaining dedicated to the *Circle of Why* keeps me focused. The temptation to fall out of sync often occurs when a coach's need to win becomes greater than the need to teach reputable morals and good character. The circle is beginning to develop sharp edges when an athlete is allowed to play because of great skill even though he or she demonstrates poor judgment and is unpleasant to be around.

> *God is far more interested in what you are*
> *than in what you do.*
> —RICK WARREN, THE PURPOSE DRIVEN LIFE

As a trainer and/or coach, you have to prove yourself just as the athletes do. As the old saying goes, lead by example. Engage an athlete in positive experiences and surround them with positive people. Youth initially become involved in my programs because they aspire to be better athletes and want my instruction in training and conditioning. What they will soon find out is my programming is much more than sweat. There is a faithful piece to what I instill which involves giving back to the community and living with good moral character.

> *We have to humble ourselves and the way*
> *you do that is by serving other people.*
> —TIM TEBOW, FORMER FOOTBALL PLAYER,
> HEISMAN TROPHY WINNER,
> MOTIVATIONAL SPEAKER

I recently was listening to a recorded lecture where motivational speaker, pastor and famed vocal artist, Wintley Phipps, was speaking on what he calls the 4G's. As I listened I began having an Oprah Winfrey, *"Aha!"* moment. Pastor Phipps was referring to exactly what I have been doing for years when training young athletes. In *Moments of Destiny,* he breaks down the 4G's as:

Giving Thanks

Gratitude

The Gift of Giving Back

The Gift of Paying it Forward

I stress the importance of family with all of the athletes I work with. A young teen showing disrespect to a parent will not be tolerated. Undesirable behaviors and bad language will be turned into lessons of appreciation and respectable conversation. One of my re-affirming messages is to always give thanks to those in your life.

A few years ago I received a phone call from a parent I was familiar with as her daughter had been on sport teams of mine in the past. This mom was anxious about the undesirable direction her daughter's life had taken in recent months. She had become disrespectful, was using foul language and ignoring schoolwork which was affecting her grades. Mom hoped her daughter's interest in trying out for my sport team meant I could guide her in a new, more positive direction.

When the young lady showed up for the first practice I asked her to leave the room and instructed her to complete a series of exercises she would find challenging. She never questioned my request, as deep down, or maybe not so deep, she knew that somehow, someway, I had learned of her changed attitude and behaviors. She had become inconsiderate and callous with a tough-girl persona, yet the body language I observed exposed a teen who was vulnerable and insecure. I worked with this young lady throughout the season, developing her physical skills, but also nurturing her mind and spirit. The obscene language ceased and her grades improved dramatically. Lack of self-esteem or a distorted perception of circumstances can often mask itself as cruel or disobedient behavior. In reality that person may be sad, frustrated, lacking confidence or confused. Mid-season, her mother sent me a message thanking me for bringing her daughter back. Things were much better at home and profanity had been replaced with "please" and "thank you." For this young woman, it was about learning to appreciate, to give thanks, to prioritize the importance of family and to believe in herself.

Gratitude comes first through prayer. Following prayer, there are countless numbers of ways to express or display signs of appreciation, for countless reasons. Be Proactive. Take the initiative and demonstrate to someone, in even the simplest of ways, just how thankful you are.

I am grateful to God for every day I am on this earth and wake up every morning prepared to tell him so. I speak to no one before I speak to God. I do not make an unnecessary spectacle of myself when I pray, but thoughtful appreciation of God is a part of my daily routine and one I share with all of the youth I work with. It is very common for the athletes I coach to pray before every game as a group. It is just what I believe ought to be done.

A few weeks ago I received a text message from a parent, not uncommon as I communicate with parents regularly. But this unexpected text touched me in its kindness and appreciation, as it was from a parent I had only recently become acquainted with. My feelings when I received this message reminded me of just how powerful gratitude can be. It began with "Pete, we were meant to meet. U are awesome with those kids. God is good and I do BELIEVE." With a few more sentences in between, the message concluded with "God knew I needed a guardian angel here on earth. Then u appeared. Crazy!!!!." Maybe not so crazy after all. I believe there is no such thing as a coincidence. Everything that happens is a part of God's bigger plan.

> *It is more blessed to give than to receive.*
> —Acts 20:35

It is very important to teach young, impressionable teens the importance of giving back to their community. I routinely have teens volunteer with charitable organizations, donate time, donate food, and raise money by collecting bottles and cans, labels or one of the other collectible fundraisers. A favorite give-back is performing small or random acts of kindness that will make an unexpected smile appear on someone's face. It's learning the importance of giving back.

> *Service to others is the rent you pay*
> *for your room here on earth.*
> —Muhammad Ali,
> Former Professional Boxer

When my athletes volunteer in the community it often involves time at a local children's hospital, the local VA hospital or a place where others, for whatever reason, might be lonely or in need of support. The lesson is about making a difference in someone's life, learning to express compassion, empathy and kindheartedness; learning to ask: "What do you need?" or, "How can I help?" It's about learning to pay it forward. Pastor and author Rick Warren writes: "The greatest gift you can give someone is your time."

I believe in inspiring young athletes. I believe in giving each of them the tools necessary to embark on a journey to sync mind, body and spirit and become the best athlete they can be, but, more importantly, to become the best person they can be. I want each of them to develop into a person of good character, a contributing member of society who has learned the value of giving back—a faithful person who understands that ultimately, God is in control.

CHAPTER TWO

Can you teach me how to dunk?

BREANNA STEWART IS ON TRACK to become the greatest female basketball player in the world, and quite possibly of all time. And, like so many other great athletes before her, this success didn't happen overnight. Breanna's exceptional journey is clearly one from which legends are made. But with every legend, with every superstar, with every Olympic champion, there is a beginning, that time in the early years when those closest to a promising athlete help nurture their vision and seek out ways to nurture potential talent. That time, for Breanna, was when she was a complete unknown. This chapter is the tale of yesteryear. One might wonder how the winner of an ESPY (Excellence in Sports Performance Yearly) Award for Best Female College Athlete, as well as dozens of other prestigious awards and honors can continue to remain so unassuming. After all, the ESPY Award is ESPN Sports equivalent to winning an Oscar at the Academy Awards, proof positive Breanna is the real deal. What you see is what you get. She is grounded. She is having fun. She is synced for success.

Breanna was in eighth grade when a transformation of sorts began to take place. Throughout her childhood she had always loved to play basketball. In middle school she donned a pair of headphones and began a routine of dribbling around her block, a routine that would remain steadfast and become incredibly valuable. As a lanky young teenager with a developing wingspan, who several years later would be humorously compared to that of a Boeing 747 by ESPN commentators, she began joining her dad to play basketball at the local YMCA. Pickup games would include guys of every age and athletic ability, but regardless of their ability, they were all competitive and showed up to play, and play hard. If there had been an initial naysayer, or less than enthusiastic reaction to having Breanna play, those thoughts vanished abruptly. The "be nice, she's a girl" scenario never played out. Breanna quickly, yet humbly, earned a deep respect from those men at the Y as she proved she could handle herself very well. In fact the guys actually looked forward to playing with her. A future star was beginning to emerge. Humility would later be a word used regularly by every media outlet imaginable when describing this phenom, but at this moment, the future face of women's collegiate basketball was preparing to enter the ninth grade.

As her eighth grade school year progressed, I began hearing more about this young female athlete who was quite a basketball player for her age. Breanna had tried out for, and made, the varsity team, but was not yet a prominent player. Breanna also participated in after-school pickup basketball games that were part of an intramural program at her junior high school. It was here I decided to stop by and see her for myself. There were no set rosters and teams were co-ed. Players were grouped by simply dividing up whoever appeared on a given day. The squads would have fun playing until the bell rang and it was time to go. Her arm span was noticeable, and for a young teen who had yet to receive any intensive coaching or training, she could capably handle the ball. There was a presence about her that led my mind to drift off a bit and imagine the what-if possibilities and the potential talent this young athlete might actually possess. The realization of just how special she would become was not even a blip on the radar.

AT THAT EARLY STAGE, BREANNA'S WINGSPAN WAS MORE LIKE THE SMALLER 737 AIRCRAFT

Breanna still had some growing to do to attain what would be become her own celebrated 7'1"-wingspan but, nevertheless, her own journey was about to take flight.

A few months after my stop at her basketball intramural program, I was coaching a group of athletes at the New York Empire State Games Track and Field Events. I had a little free time and decided to head over to the indoor venue and watch some basketball. As I sat in the bleachers, I noticed Breanna was a player on one of the regional teams in the games, so, as destiny continued to knock on our doors, I was able to watch her play in a more competitive environment than I had previously observed. During that game, I had a casual conversation with Breanna's dad, Brian, that was more of an ice breaker than a serious discussion. Nonetheless, a connection was made. Soon after that, another encounter with Breanna cemented our bond. While we were both in the local high school weight room, Breanna walked up to me with the uninhibited and unpretentious zeal of a young teen on a mission, and asked if I would be her trainer. Without a pause, she continued to talk, adding yet another question to her first query. "Oh, yeah, and can you teach me how to dunk?" Her passion for the sport was undeniable and this was not a chance meeting, it was part of a bigger plan. My answer to both questions was "Yes!"

And so began the transformation from a tall, long limbed, gangly girl into an athlete. Not just any athlete, but a premiere athlete whose dream was to someday become the new face of women's basketball—and the new face of Nike. Her dreams were big. She was a girl who wanted to win basketball championships, a girl who, in a few short years, would hold her fate in her hands, having already accumulated numerous gold medals and prestigious state and national awards. A girl who, while still in her teens would grace the March, 2014, cover of *Sports Illustrated* magazine.

Breanna's nickname was Bre, and it was by this moniker that she was most commonly addressed while in high school. In college she would adopt the nickname, Stewie, (as well as a few others) but for now it was still Bre. And for me it will always remain Bre. Before our decision to train together, Bre had played on a few teams and participated in recreational basketball programs, but my type of training would be a new experience for her. I was, theoretically, her strength and conditioning coach, but her training with me would be much more profound. It was not my job to teach the fundamental skills of passing and shooting, strategy and X's and O's, there were other wonderful coaches to whom those jobs would fall. Bre and I needed to start at the very beginning to build a foundation based on the development and synchronization of her mind, body and spirit. Becoming a champion wouldn't be based on physical prowess alone. Daily sessions in the weight room working on coordination, strength and endurance would certainly be a part of her training. Just as important was developing a mental picture of who she could become and learning to believe that she could get there.

IT WASN'T ABOUT *IF* BREANNA WOULD BECOME A CHAMPION; IT WAS ABOUT *WHEN*

It was the mental preparation that would ultimately convince her she is the best player in the country. Emblazoned in her psyche would be the belief that she could, and would, achieve whatever she put her mind to.

Later in this book is a chapter titled *Perception vs. Reality* (page 51). In this chapter, I share a compilation of assessments I use with potential athletes. The concept is to uncover the variety of ways players identify themselves mentally and physically with regard to their level of athletic ability, and to dig down to their true attitude, their real priorities.

Humility versus Narcissism

Authenticity versus Disingenuousness

Perception versus Reality

The process often offers a bit of a surprise for many young aspiring athletes when ego collides with fact. There is typically a lot of bloviating about great skill, possession of superior equipment and statements referencing one's willingness to live and breathe whatever their favorite sport is, but as you will read in that chapter, those are not the answers I seek.

Ability may get you to the top,
but it takes character to keep you there.
—JOHN WOODEN, BASKETBALL COACH

One of the first tasks I ventured into with Bre was a road trip to a local reservoir that is used by athletic teams from many schools in the area for training. An open grassy hillside descends from all around the reservoir with fencing that surrounds the actual tanks. The north end of the reservoir's hillside is a tall, long slope, and it is here this test always begins. The distance from the bottom of the hill to the fencing at the top is approximately seven hundred feet. The elevation at the hill's peak is six hundred twenty-three feet. The goal is to run the inclined distance in forty-five seconds, or less, with two minutes allotted to descend the slope, regroup and repeat the task again. It is not unusual to see kids throwing up after the first or second set, while others are unable to finish because of a leg cramp and still more drop out of the drill without completing even the first rotation as their times are well below the set standard. As a young aspiring athlete, discovering that your current perception of your athletic proficiency may have been slightly, or drastically, miscalculated is often a disappointing lesson in the realities of life. Nevertheless, it is a valuable experiential lesson that is necessary to learn and grow.

For this particular trip to the reservoir I grouped Bre with several male athletes I was also training. These athletes were currently competing at the college and professional level. One of the athletes was among the top prep school quarterbacks in the country. Another was a player with the Baltimore Ravens. All of the athletes were in good shape, but this was a test for those reaching for the next level. All of the participants completed two laps, and a few started falling off after three. The remainder of the guys finished four rounds, which was respectable. Then they watched in disbelief as Bre continued past lap five to six. The entire time she never wavered from the standard that had been set at forty-five seconds up and no more than two minutes down. At the end of lap six, Breanna stopped. She commented her legs felt heavy but she was okay. I already knew Bre was competitive and self-driven, but on that day she began to experience the results that can be attained when mind and body are aligned for a common goal. She was humble, authentic, and her perception was reality.

PREPARE YOUR MIND FOR ANYTHING

Most coaches will agree that you become what you are in the weight room. With Bre that was true as well, but the weight room was not just about weight machines and cardio. It needed to be, and to this day remains, more than just a workout. The weights and machines are her competition. It's not about a cookie-cutter weight program geared for a particular position an athlete may play on the field or court. It's about the individual.

Since I began working with Bre, a core focus of her training has always been longevity—longevity for sustainable performance in each game, and longevity in her continued good health and the length of her athletic career. The objective was to create and maintain an endurance level that would enable her to play an entire game without getting tired, as well as the capability to sprint down the court and routinely be one of the first team mates offensively positioned, ready for a pass. This level is not often mastered with such perfection by the taller, bigger players.

Bre trained with precision and followed the demanding, somewhat unconventional, protocol I developed for her. The goal was to keep her lean and fast. Though some would comment she was too thin and needed to bulk up, bulk would slow her down, and negatively impact all that we had worked to accomplish. She attained the high-aerobic capacity I was seeking, and maximized her ability to run up and down the hardwoods like a gazelle. Spectators, coaches and athletes alike can enjoy watching the phenomenal results of Bre's hard work and faithful commitment to the game she loves. She has a dedicated allegiance to herself and to the teams she plays with. It doesn't take a crystal ball to see the best is yet to come.

BREANNA WON HER FIRST TEAM USA BASKETBALL CHAMPIONSHIP AT THE AGE OF 14

Bre was in the ninth grade when she brought a letter in for me to read. It was an invitation from the USA Women's Basketball Organization to try out for the U16 team that would be competing that year in Mexico. Initially, her plan was to train for one more year while continuing to play ball locally. Having received the invite, it was time to rethink her course of action. Though her parents were initially reluctant, conversations with me and others eased their concerns. With her parents' support, she accepted the invitation and made the squad. At age 14 she was the youngest member of the team that went on to win the gold medal.

When still in high school, Bre's dad would often stop by the weight room where she was working out. Her strength and conditioning program was now year-round. As well as playing on her school team and with various other local groups, she remained a contender with the USA Women's Basketball Program. On this visit, her dad expressed concern about Bre advancing through the next round of cuts for the USA team that would be heading to France. She was going to be competing against some extremely talented athletes, stronger and tougher than what her competition had been at the previous year's tryouts. The best players in her age group from across the country would be gathering under one roof with the same hope of being chosen for a coveted spot on the team. I turned to Bre who had been listening and simply asked, "Do you have this?" Without hesitation she responded "I've got this, coach." Her dad remained a bit anxious thinking about what remained ahead and the pressure Bre must be feeling. But Bre was calm, relaxed and confident. Not egotistically confident, I would not have allowed that, but unpretentiously confident. Her dad was familiar with the physical aspect of my training with Bre, but he was still learning just how focused and self assured Bre was becoming.

Bre went on to make the cut and her USA Basketball Team came home from Europe with another gold medal. I received a phone call from France as Bre's proud parents watched her accept the gold. Her father said three words and hung up the phone. He said "I Get It." He now understood the foundation of my training and that it was more than just a strength and conditioning workout. There was a reason that by the end of her sophomore year she was rated the number-one high school player in the country. But not just any number-one player, she was being compared to a small group of legendary women's basketball players who had preceded her. Success in syncing Bre's mind, body and spirit was about to reach new heights.

BREANNA WON TEAM USA BASKETBALL AWARDS HER FRESHMAN, SOPHOMORE, JUNIOR AND SENIOR YEARS OF HIGH SCHOOL

To videotape or not to videotape while I was training Bre was never much of a question. I will occasionally film an athlete practicing, or playing during a game, but I've never really found videotaping valuable as a tool for assessing my training goals. In recent years though, I have implemented the routine use of a program many coaches, trainers and athletes find beneficial. The software is called Dartfish and it can be used to easily break down and analyze movements, categorize videos, and catalog information for easy reference. The software uses digital video graphics to deliver instant visual feedback. Dartfish is an effective and results-driven analytical database that I find incredibly useful for the athletes I work with. Pieces of information are like a puzzle continually being augmented and adjusted seeking biomechanical body movements that lead to optimal performance. With Bre, Dartfish has also been a cinematographic delight, as sometimes I am able to capture moves that are sheer delight to watch.

Bre rarely questions why or what she is being asked to do during training. She works hard and never complains. But, as with any teen, there are always exceptions. At this point in her career, Bre's high school basketball team was on target to win the New York State Championships. This would be a back-to-back success as her team, under the direction of head coach Eric Smith, went on to win the title that season and the following year. Bre was also training for a position on the upcoming years USA Basketball Team. Consistent training was essential. I had scheduled a weight room training that Bre was supposed to attend prior to a Friday night football game. It was clear she was to train first and then go to the game. As any teenager under peer pressure from her friends, Bre called me before the game and asked if she could hang out with her buddies and go straight to the game. After all, it was Friday night. In retrospect this was a turning point in her decision-making maturity, dedication and loyalty. I hung up the phone and sat down to wait. The choice would be hers. Soon after our phone call, Bre walked in to the weight room. She looked at me for a reaction, a comment, anything, but I spoke not a word. She quietly began her work out.

A wise person knows that sometimes
silence speaks volumes.
—UNKNOWN

There was no need to shout, humiliate or lecture. That isn't my style. Bre didn't bother to question what I was thinking, as my silence was her answer. At the end of the workout Bre said, "Thank you," as she did at the end of every workout, and left. Yes, she missed some time with her friends before the game that Friday night, but that decision, as small as it seemed at the time, helped to cement the foundation and work ethic upon which her future would be built.

Breanna was becoming a bigger blip on the radar as she continued to accumulate prestigious awards including the Gatorade New York Girls' Basketball Player of the Year in 2011. Nevertheless she remained focused and driven, having already developed a plan. She knew her agenda would take years to achieve, but she was determined to whittle away at it, continuing to accomplish each set of milestones in the climb to her zenith. That high point would be making the USA women's national team playing for the FIBA World Cup and going on to the 2016 Olympics in Rio de Janeiro.

Months passed and one evening before practice, Bre showed up with a new pair of sneakers, expensive sneakers she had recently worn when playing for her USA basketball team. She was proud of her sneakers and rightfully so. But I also knew she was a bit vulnerable with her new found celebrity status. Bre's strength was hard work and authenticity; vanity would need to be checked at the door. Did I really believe a pair of sneakers would in any way compromise what we had worked to attain up to this point? No, but I wasn't going to take any chances. The ground remained wet from a recent shower, and, though I hadn't quite made up my mind where she would run her practice that day, my decision had just been made. Since those were the sneakers she had brought to practice, those were the shoes she would wear outside to run on the grass still muddy from the rain. Do athletes need to wear clothing and footwear that is safe and appropriate for competition? Absolutely. The sneakers were not so much the issue as her attitude at that moment about how perfect and clean they were. The line was blurred between focus on the material and hard work. This line needed a re-clarification. Bre was not even close to the goals she aspired to, so celebrating greatness would have to wait. To me they were just a very nice pair of sneakers that were about to get very dirty. My mother would always tell me, "God frowns on those who worship material things." And I believe that to this day. Yes, one can wear team clothing they have earned and celebrate a win. But don't get caught up in glitzy popularity and self-worth.

REMAIN UNPRETENTIOUS, AND STILL HAVE A GREAT REPUTATION

Brianna wears specialty T-shirts with championship titles, and other accolades that she has certainly earned the right to wear. But she remains humble and focused. There is always room for growth and she knows she has not yet reached the pinnacle of her career. As a teenager, it is often difficult to keep an ego in check. Even with her rising superstar status, she still remembers where she came from. Bre helps out at hometown events with the same passion she exhibits at her ever-growing list of high profile occasions, and still waits her turn for a machine when she comes into her old high school weight room to work out.

When working with Bre in high school she always gave her best. Bre was also, and continues to be, recognized as a genuine team player. But sometimes it was necessary to just let kids be kids and break loose. A favorite place for Breanna and her friends to go and relax was the buffet at an event center located about thirty miles away. When we arrived I would remind them of the one rule everyone had to follow: No one could talk about or mention the word basketball. The mission of the evening was to eat as much as you could consume, be teens and laugh. A kind of spiritual re-grouping. It was about letting go and having fun. Literally, food for the soul.

In March of 2012, Bre received the Gatorade National Girls' Basketball Player of the Year Award. She would go on to receive the Gatorade Female Athlete of the Year. She would leave high school a basketball star. Hers is a legacy for up and coming athletes to look up to and learn from. Bre entered UCONN as a freshman in the fall of 2012. I watched Bre play through the 2013 finals of the Women's NCAA Championships. UCONN would win and Bre would be selected as the Tournament's Most Outstanding Player. In 2014 I watched again as Nashville, Tennessee, hosted the Women's Final Four. UCONN won yet another national championship and Breanna scored her second straight MOP award. In 2015 it was a three-peat as UCONN controlled the court once again, this time at Tampa Bay. UCONN took home yet another championship and Bre was awarded her third consecutive Tournament MOP.

As Bre has gotten older, many watching her play say she moves like Kevin Durant, referring to her as the female version of this excitable superstar. Emma Carmichael wrote in *Sports Illustrated* (3/24/14), "She is the Kevin Durant of Women's Basketball." Reciprocally, Bre has been a longtime fan of Durant himself. At the 2014 ESPY awards she was moments away from having the opportunity to meet Kevin on the red carpet when she was unexpectedly swept away to receive her own award, Best Female College

Athlete. I am sure there will be a time in the not-so-distant future when their paths will cross again. In a recent issue of "ESPN The Magazine," (11/14), Durant is quoted as saying, "Breanna Stewart is the real deal, ... She's something we've never seen before."

Bre has played against WNBA players who are very impressed with her talent. Diana Taurasi, basketball superstar and UCONN alumni, has said Breanna would be her number one draft pick if there were a draft today. Rebecca Loba (*Yahoo Sports* 3/19/14) has said if Stewart were to declare for the WNBA draft this season, she would be the first pick because of her skills and because she's only getting better. Bre is in line to win the largest number of gold medals of any player in Women's USA Basketball Team history. In September 2014, Brianna was, indeed, selected to the USA women's national team. Playing for the FIBA World Cup, Brianna and her squad brought home yet another gold medal. As milestones continue to be reached, one of the few factors currently separating Brianna from attaining her biggest dream, the 2016 Olympics, is simply time.

Breanna is in a positive place and has fun when she plays basketball. And yes, she's had her first dunk. Her superstar status continues to intensify and her media presence continues to expand. I have taught Bre how to sync her mind, body and spirit; to remain humble and selfless, regardless of the circumstances. Her family is her mainstay. As her fame increases and that 747 behemoth of an athlete soars to new heights I will continue to train her in the off-season and check in regularly with the same recurring question: "Do you have this?" It is a simple, yet powerful question that represents a code of sorts. "I've got this coach. "

CHAPTER THREE

For I know the plans I have for you

THIS CHAPTER IS ABOUT BRYCE MOORE, my son. And unlike what you might be thinking at this point, this chapter is not a proud father bloviating about the special talents his son possesses, or overstating the same dreams and aspirations so many young athletes and their parents may share. It's about a journey. A plan established by a much higher power than myself and one my wife, son and I remain faithfully drawn to. It is a journey of patience, gratitude, effort and prayer.

> *With your efforts steady and consistent,*
> *have the patience to let life unfold*
> *at a sustainable pace. The results you seek*
> *will surely come to you in good time.*
> —PHIL WEBB, CONSULTANT

Bryce was less than twelve months old when I used to take his little arms in mine and simulate the motion of throwing a basketball. Just as listening to music in a mother's womb is intended to stimulate the brain's potential, I decided there was no harm in practicing movements that could, potentially, have positive implications later in life. And it was cute!

As a preschooler, I bought Bryce a Little Tikes® basketball hoop. I enjoyed teaching him the basic shots, and we had fun. At that same time, Bryce started to go to the weight room with me while I was training other athletes. I explained the various machines to Bryce and what each of their general purposes was. In no time, Bryce was following me around the training area, correcting athletes as well as a preschooler could, joyfully smiling as he simulated a mini me. Bryce didn't come to every training practice, that would have been unprofessional, but when he did arrive on the scene it reminded everyone in the room of what their first priority should always remain regardless of their goals—family.

The Little Tikes basketball hoop continued to shift up the height adjustments and by the age of 5 we were at the last notch. By age 6, Bryce was practicing on a standard size hoop and my wife and I were playing little basketball games incorporating screening, passing and shooting skills. Like thousands, maybe millions, of other kids, he now aspired to be Michael Jordan. When Bryce looked in the mirror he didn't see a little kid, he saw a legend. He saw the greatest basketball player of all time. He envisioned himself in that jersey wearing number twenty-three.

DREAM BIG

One night while we were out browsing through a local sporting goods store, Bryce came upon a regulation size portable basketball hoop set up for customers to view and try. So, Bryce began shooting. Bryce also began making shots. Not just the first, second and third shot but the fourth, fifth, sixth and more. A small crowd of customers and employees gathered around and were a bit amazed at what they saw. After all, the kid was only 6 years old. He finally missed a shot, which was bound to happen, but Bryce, and quite honestly my wife and I, were savoring those few seconds of excitement. Every parent thinks his or her kid is special and at that moment I was experiencing a flash of what was to come.

There is an arcade in this same mall, as there is in most, which had a basketball shooting game. Bryce was just as consistent at this game as he was on a standard hoop and his scores would draw a curious crowd of youth. Not so much for the scores alone, but for the fact it was a child who had yet to clear 4' in height making the shots. One evening while enjoying a break from the arcade in the food court area Bryce looked at my wife and I and proclaimed he would be playing on television one day. At that time his imaginary TV debut was as a basketball player. Little did we know that dream would come true, just not in that sport.

Bryce was still playing basketball in the driveway when I signed him up with a local YMCA league that other coaches and their sons were a part of. The league was excellent, but I wanted to test the waters and give Bryce the opportunity to try a variety of sports, particularly ones that involved more running. Bryce had played soccer at the YMCA as a preschooler, so I re-enrolled him in the local Y soccer league. Right-footed kicking was the norm, particularly at his age, but I worked with Bryce on kicking with equal consistency using both his left and right foot. This task should have seemed a bit uncoordinated and awkward at first, but he developed the balance of sides rather easily. Two particular kids on his team were good soccer players and Bryce enjoyed playing with them, but mid-season they both left the team to play baseball. The team really needed to come together, meshing basic skill strengths with position play—and come together they did. Bryce scored a couple of goals, using his left foot no less, and, with his team united, the team won the championship game. It was an early lesson in the old saying, "There is no I in team."

During the soccer off-season, Bryce and I decided karate might be a fun and challenging experience. Bryce understood and appreciated the discipline involved with karate and the emphasis placed on self development. Fundamentals such as attitude, perseverance, and gratitude were in line with my own philosophical mind set when training athletes. But athletically, it just didn't speak to him. Karate, though physically challenging, was too sedentary for Bryce. He wanted to run.

> *Be thankful that you can savor the process*
> *of working your way toward a meaningful goal.*
> —RALPH MARSTON, WRITER AND
> PUBLISHER OF THE DAILY MOTIVATOR

At age 6, our next stop was Little League® Tee Ball. Tee Ball was a bit slow paced for Bryce, but he stuck with it through the season. The majority of the kids were there for the ice cream after the game, and that was okay— Bryce liked ice cream as well. Coaches put the players on the field, spread them out and let them have fun.

The next season would be Little League and honestly I couldn't wait. Registration day arrived and over I drove to sign my son up. I was one happy dad. As we started to get out of the car I heard his sweet voice ask in the politest of tones, "Dad, would it be okay if I played soccer one more year?" A feeling of disappointment rushed through me like a river breaking through a dam, but I had to conceal my initial reaction. My responding question was simple "Is soccer what you want to do, son?" "Yes, dad." And we got back in the car and drove away. My initial disappointment turned to joy in reflection as I thought to myself, thank you, God, for giving my son the ability to know it is okay to ask.

Conversations about nothing are often stepping stones to conversations of substance. Since my son was old enough to speak, we have talked. I don't wait for conversations to be just about discipline, chores, grades or expectations, in fact our conversations are often frivolous and lighthearted. The point is, we talk. Our dialogue is grounded in communication, not question and answer. Communication that will hopefully evolve into a life skill that can be used both personally and professionally. In this case, my son had thought about his choices and expressed his feelings. Not bad for a soon-to-be 7-year-old. Though I may initially have been a bit disappointed, in the end I was very proud.

Year two of soccer season began. At the same time, Bryce's recreational interest at home was shifting from basketball to baseball. The hoop was still being used regularly and Michael Jordan remained Bryce's favorite athlete, but more time was being consumed in backyard batting practice. We were working on batting basics and starting to practice switch hitting. I had put together a ball on a string and attached it to a bat similar to the wooden paddle and elastic attached rubber ball you see in toy departments. I would soft toss the ball to him, a standard drill that involves standing near the batter and tossing the ball underhand to build batting skills. He was hooked and I was starting to realize his batting potential. The next year he decided he really wanted to join Little League.

RESPECT THE CONVERSATION, EVEN IF YOU DON'T AGREE WITH THE MESSAGE

Bryce was as impressionable as any child his age, and one of the first groups of coaches he encountered at Little League had that in-your-face style. What they were encouraging Bryce to do was in direct contradiction to what I was teaching him at home and Bryce would get frustrated—rightfully so. Regardless of differing adult viewpoints, I told my son, "Whatever the coach says, you listen. You don't have to agree but you do have to listen." We would talk about what the coach said when we returned home. The lesson was respect. At that moment Bryce was to do what the coach told him to do, whether he agreed or disagreed, as it was about showing consideration for the adult speaking to you.

The coach's guidance typically involved routine advice and an ordinary strategy, which was bearable at the time. What bothered me the most was that he was discouraging Bryce from batting left-handed. Switch hitting was something I had worked on with Bryce for over a year and he was good at it. An unusual skill-set was not going to be considered by this coach. It was clear any attempt at switch hitting would disrupt a routine that had probably been in place for some time. The situation boiled down to the politics of sport, something any parent involved in youth sport, or any aged sport for that matter, can probably relate to. It was the good, the bad, and the ugly.

> *Hindsight is always 20/20.*
> —BILLY WILDER, FILMMAKER

To exacerbate the situation I would start to coach Bryce from the side-lines. My vision for Bryce was long-term and to me it seemed reasonable to experiment with strategies and test skill basics. Bryce was comfortable batting both sides and I was trying to establish a foundation for future success. I was frustrated by a coach telling my son what he couldn't do rather than what he could and in hindsight my frustration probably came across as a bit of arrogance. I was not practicing what I preached and was reacting rather than being proactive. I was told my son wasn't the talent I claimed him to be, and that possibly I was being too tough on him. I decided it was time to move on. It was time to focus on what Bryce can do, rather than what he can't. Keep moving forward. Just keep moving forward.

> *Life's mishaps are only a page*
> *out of a grand book. Be patient in affliction.*
> —MAX LUCADO, THE WOODCUTTER'S WISDOM

We were on a family vacation at Disney World when Bryce, at age 8, made another one of his visionary statements. "Dad, I want to play on these fields one day." He was referring to the Disney Wide World of Sports complex. I obliged him as I did with all his dreams, and we returned home. Home, to begin a new venture with travel baseball.

For those readers that aren't quite sure of what the difference is between a Little League team and a travel baseball team I will give you the short version. Little League teams, though structured by the organizations national guidelines, are typically organized and controlled locally. Games are typically in fairly close proximity or often in the same sports complex. There is a set seasonal schedule. Travel teams can play upwards of 50 games a year and typically train year-round. There is a much bigger opportunity for tournament play, and a greater chance for exposure to scouts, and coaches, as well as college and professional organizations. The cost and time commitment can both be very high.

OPEN A CHILD'S MIND, LET THEM MAKE MISTAKES, LET THEM LEARN

Bryce enjoyed travel baseball and though the schedule was a bit crazy, he was able to manage his time well. Team politics continued as usual and players with less talent would frequently be placed ahead of Bryce in the line-up. Whether it was to spite me or Bryce I'm not sure. But, as a young player, he was still learning about himself as well as the sport. From a coach, words like can't and don't are powerful messages for an impressionable young man. I didn't want negative feedback to make him feel like he wasn't good enough or couldn't achieve the milestones he was striving for. I didn't want to close opportunities that might exist or to break his spirit.

I began to question my own vision. Had I been overzealous in assessing my son's talent? Kids believe what adults say. Were the coaches, players and parents who said Bryce wasn't going to be good, or was doing it wrong, targeting Bryce, or were they aiming those negative comments at me? It was time to take Bryce to events outside of the area for an unbiased view of his talent.

I AM BATMAN

No, this wasn't a comparison to the Caped Crusader who protected Gotham City and rescued innocent victims from unusually colorful villains. Bryce had picked up the nickname, Batman, as a result of the number of bats he was accumulating. While other 9-year-old boys yearned to possess the newest action figures and other hot playthings on the market, Bryce was continually on the prowl for the latest bat. He was currently using a regular aluminum bat, but that was all about to change.

Bryce was 10 when I placed a call to Under Armour (UA) about baseball training. The person I spoke with said he was too young but they would make an exception. So, off we drove to Maryland, hub of the UA Baseball Factory Organization. While Bryce was being videotaped, the attending coach was giving him performance cues. Bryce was hitting okay, but there seemed to be a disconnect between Bryce and what the coach was trying to communicate. I had been working on his swing mechanics for some time now: his stance, loading phase, timing, launch and follow-through. Through time we had developed our own jargon. "Tell him to flip his hips," I yelled out. The coach did, and Bryce began striking the ball with flawless perfection. After giving a raised eyebrow to me, and inquiring about my history, he said Bryce was the best kid he had ever seen swing for his age. The coach went on to say Bryce's performance was spectacular and he was talented well beyond his years.

GOD'S GLORIOUS UNFOLDING

Back home, a major tournament was going to take place in Cooperstown, New York. The travel team Bryce was currently on had been invited to play in the tournament, but Bryce had his sights set on participating in the Home Run Derby, one of the most exciting events taking place that weekend. Home Run Derby's are a contest where players get ten chances to hit the ball as well and as far as they can. The batter can hit right-handed, left-handed or both. It is the preeminent event for young baseball players.

Before the actual competition, Bryce had to go to a tryout. A few weeks before the event an evaluation of his hitting took place at a facility closer to home. Bryce typically warmed up for batting as if he were going to be switch hitting so he would practice swinging both right- and left- handed. One of the coaches watching him warm up commented to me that I shouldn't be pushing him to bat left-handed, he would just get cut. I pondered his point for a few moments and respectfully disagreed. Would this coach later be proven false? Absolutely, but not before Bryce learned a valuable lesson in God's timing.

During that same stretch of time, our travels landed us at a UA training camp in Maryland where Bryce's ability blended well with the 14- and 15-year-old players he had been matched up with. Taking a moment to think back just a few short years, it became clear our decision to keep moving forward, in spite of those pessimistic people early on, had been the right choice to make.

Like a dotted line crossing the country on a map, we then found ourselves in Buffalo, New York, where Bryce played on an all-star team at the Cal Ripkin State Championship finals. Next stop, Delaware, where Bryce hit a shot two hundred seventy four feet. Impressive, to say the least.

Bryce came home thinking he would be invited to participate in the upcoming home run derby at the invite-only event in Cooperstown. After all, with the exception of one coach who disagreed with my switch-hitting concept, recent feedback from prominent trainers had been very positive.

Bryce went to Cooperstown with his team and upon his arrival was told the decision as to who would fill the final spot in the derby was down to him and one other player. They would compete against each other and whoever did best would be in the derby competition. Their abilities where equally matched and even those judging said the decision was very difficult, but in the end, this time around it wasn't meant to be. Bryce would watch the derby competition from the bleachers and, like so many of us do in times of disappointment or sadness, he wondered, "Why?"

Bryce had always prayed every night before he went to bed, but frustration was building up and leading him to ask "Why?" I remember him saying "I work so hard, dad. If I'm not going to play well, what is the point in praying?" My response would be repeated a few times, as it takes awhile for kids to understand. Frustration clouded his vision and he wanted an answer right then, but eventually the message became clear.

> *You are being tested.*
>
> *Do you only pray when you want something?*
>
> *Prayer should be continual.*
>
> *God will answer when you pray and*
> *place unconditional trust in God's plan.*

I reinforced to him that he definitely had the potential and reflected on all the good things that had happened up to this point. We discussed all he had accomplished, and the adversity he had overcome. God was just saying it wasn't his time. Bryce needed to continue walking the journey God had planned and put his trust in the Lord.

> *God will make you shine when the time is right.*

The following year, Bryce was invited to participate in the National Home Run Derby in Albany New York. He not only won the Stars and Stripes Derby, but he won batting left-handed (he batted his first five right-handed and then switched to left), an accomplishment naysayers said couldn't be done. His team also went on to win the 2011 Winter Wood Bat Tournament. Just a few months later Bryce was chosen to play on the team that would go on to win the 12-year-old division of the USSA National Wooden Bat World Series Championships in Kissimmee, Florida. The various teams Bryce was a member of were becoming known for tournament play and winning.

Bryce was 12 when he returned to another UA Baseball Factory housed in Kansas. I handed him a 33" wood bat. Typically at that age kids are using a 30-31" bat. He batted left- and right-handed. The assessment given by the representatives was that he was hitting better than most high school players. Accompanying the UA coaches at this event was a coach of major league baseball player Albert Pujols, an All-Star and World Series champion, who commented specifically on my son's talent. It was interesting to see other players who had been watching Bryce, and who were using aluminum bats, switch to try wood. But then again, Bryce was Batman. And I had a theory about the use of various bats.

There are basically four types of baseball bats: Alloy/metal, composite, wood and hybrid.

The type of bat suggested for use varies. Youth bats typically feature a 2¼" (small) barrel diameter and are often lighter in weight (usually aluminum) and average no more than 33" in length. Senior league bats have a bigger barrel and increased length. Composite bats tend to have more of a trampoline effect. BBCOR (Batted Ball Coefficient of Restitution) bats are used in college and high school baseball. The mathematical formula that makes up BBCOR focuses on how much of a trampoline effect the barrel of a bat has on a ball, in other words, how much energy is lost during the bat's contact with the ball. Bat manufacturers have to, in effect, stifle the trampoline bounce that pitched balls experience when a batter makes contact. BBCOR bats can have a barrel no larger than 2⅝" in diameter. Wood, of course, is used by professional baseball players.

Bottom line: the finished product is wood. At the end of the road, if a player makes it to the pros, they will be playing with wood. Manufacturers know bats are big business and the progression is a money maker. I suggest you start with what you will end up with: wood. With BBCOR standards, aluminum bats will theoretically be the same as wooden bats. Good news, as far as I'm concerned, for those players that must use them. For everyone else, use wood. I believe a good hitter can hit with wood. There are those who disagree, my son being one of those. Bryce likes to buy bats and though he knows logically the mechanics behind what I say is true, he wants to own a variety of bats. Score one for manufacturers marketing and impressionable kids.

DON'T LET MATERIAL ITEMS BE AN ATTEMPT TO BUY AN IDENTITY

In 2012 I formed my own travel team. We call ourselves the AOTR Junior Legends. The team is named after an organization I founded, called AOTR (Athletes On The Rise). The team is made up of athletes that train with AOTR, an organization I founded that is dedicated to the development of all athletes in all sports. Each athlete is provided individual and team instruction to develop the necessary skills and respectable character traits needed to achieve their goals. It is a positive learning environment that prepares athletes mentally and physically for the future. A friend of mine, Stephen Kuss, signed on as a coach with AOTR travel baseball and our vision began to unfold.

In two years as a team, these young men have united as a family and suc-
ceeded beyond our wildest expectations. With the creation of our team
came a new tradition—prayer. Not that prayer was new, it wasn't. It was
the way in which we were going to pray. I wanted our team to be proud
of their faith so prayer would no longer happen only in the private moments before a game as it had in the past. Prayer would happen united, in
a circle, over home plate. Bryce prayed every evening at home, something
he had done since he was a very young child, and he had been quietly
praying before every game for years. That is, in a corner by the bleachers
or another empty spot in the stadium. This would be a public display of
supplication. Being a kid, Bryce immediately questioned what the other
teams would say, what the spectators would say, what everybody would
say. I didn't care. As a team, AOTR was going to pray. The first time we
prayed together, I led the prayer. The second time I asked my son to begin.
He was embarrassed but he did it. Now he leads every prayer over home
plate before the start of a game.

Other teams may try to psych us out with their expensive uniforms, special shoes, recognized sponsor or previous big tournament wins. I still
hear, "Dad, look at their shoes, they must be better than us." Wrong, son.
AOTR comes out onto the field in basic uniforms and people recognize us
because of our record, yes, but also because of the comradery we share.
We are the team that openly prays.

> *I fear no one because of my belief in God.*
> *I am one of the Lord's children. We control*
> *what we can control. We must go out and perform*
> *rather than worry about who is the supposed best.*

The Junior Legends have won numerous elite tournaments and in June of
2014, two of my son's dreams came true. He and his team qualified to play
in the Disney International Salute to Baseball Championships. The tour-

nament was held at the same Disney complex where Bryce, as an 8-year-old, said he would play some day. The game was carried by ESPN, his TV dream come true. Eighteen elite teams competed for the much sought after trophy but AOTR came out on top, the champions. It was an aspiration Bryce had held on to, becoming reality. The team then qualified for the summer National Championships in Myrtle Beach, South Carolina, just a few weeks away. Making it as far as the semi-finals, that trophy slipped through their fingers this time around, but in the process Bryce had realized another one of life's lessons.

> *To obtain anything of great value,*
> *you must provide great value*
> *and exert great effort. Spreading that effort*
> *over a reasonable amount of time*
> *is a key to dependable success.*
> —PHIL WEBB, CONSULTANT

As I work with my son and other athletes I want to make sure they understand longevity. Becoming a premiere athlete is a process that takes years. It is formulating a foundation from which you can then develop the ability to sync your mind, body and spirit. In March of 2015, Bryce was recognized as the Showcase Player of the Month for the bat manufacturer, HeavySwing. This national recognition is given to an amateur baseball and softball player for their hard work, dedication and success, both on and off the field.

As Bryce looks ahead, he would like to attend the University of North Carolina. Yes, UNC has a fine baseball team, but it is also the alma mater of His Airness, Michael Jordan, who is still Bryce's favorite athlete. For now, Bryce and his AOTR teammates have their sights on becoming the top-ranked team in the nation. For now, only God knows the plan.

CHAPTER FOUR

Perception vs. *reality*

IT IS IMPORTANT TO DISCOVER, early in our relationship, how an athlete perceives himself or herself. It is from this perception that my training begins. Not just physical training, but guidance in how to prepare one's mind and body for identified goals, which typically include the mastery of a sport. Identifying where a novice athlete places themselves on a measure of 1 to 10 is more than a scale of posed questions and analyzed performance. My assessments are comparable to peeling away layers of an onion, removing layer upon layer of belief until at last discovering what is actually at the factual core. It is an opportunity for self-reflection and self-analysis. It's a chance to navigate the *Circle of Why*, and to clarify one's motivation and purpose. It is a screening process to vet perception and face reality, establishing in mind, body and spirit where this person truthfully is and where it is they genuinely want to be. Creating a common goal lets us create the journey to get there.

GOOD IS GOOD, BUT GOOD IS NOT GREAT

When I begin working with an athlete, establishing a sense of humility is key. I want an athlete to recognize where their talents and mindset really are, to accept that reality and to move forward. At this stage of the game 10 is fiction, not fact.

One of the first assignments I pose to aspiring athletes is to list five life priorities. Number 1 is their top priority, and number 5 is their lowest. When a kid doesn't put a parent in the top 3, there is a problem. Stating that their allegiance is to football or that they can't exist without playing soccer may seem like mere words, but it can affect their attitude. Their answers reveal a current mindset, and help me determine just how much of an adjustment needs to occur.

When priorities are misaligned it is sometimes necessary to do an awareness renovation. Breaking the person down and building them back up with realigned priorities gives them a chance to develop the characteristics of a respectable individual. It teaches them the importance of an education, an attitude of gratitude, how to show respect and the use of proper manners.

On a priority list of 1 through 5, parents and family need to be a 1. On a scale of 1 to 10, family needs to be a 10. To place God at the top is a bonus point. I can assure you that the first 10 an athlete who works with me achieves is for recognition of the importance of family and faith in their lives. I work with a diverse group of athletes, so expressions of faith may vary. But, like a stream filled with fish of many colors, it is possible for us all to swim in the same water. We learn, we share, we pray.

> *It is through faith that a righteous person has life.*
> —*ROMANS 1:17*

I have found that regional and cultural diversity will often challenge the idea of what is appropriate when it comes to family values, but in the end there should be one universally common goal: To give all children a chance to be a 10.

It is important to know an athlete on and off the field, and to develop a mutual sense of trust early on in the relationship. Who you are, and what you become begins at home. I always tell kids to tell their parents they love them every night before they go to sleep.

There is also the team family. Coaches want players to be connected like a family. And thankfully, very often that connection is made. Unfortunately, players sometimes wear sport shirts emblazoned with the word family, and they aren't connected in the least. Wearing a shirt that says family doesn't make you family. A word doesn't make people connected. A group of athletes teamed together wearing identifiable T-shirts with the word family on the back may signify the visual cohesion of a team, but it may or may not represent actual emotional unification.

In my opinion, if you are going to call a team a family you need to know them—really know them. Ask a coach about their players, particularly the less talented ones, and see what they know. Ask a teammate about another player and see how they respond. Answers will reveal the true state of a team family.

The Junior Legends travel baseball team I coach, as well as the athletes I work with through my AOTR training program, have two common chants: "All in" and "Family." Ask me about any one of the athletes I work with and I will be able to write a short story about them—any one of them. Their teammates will, too. The kids interact socially together. They understand each other and the families do things together. They go to movies, hang out, share meals and look out for each other. Core kids, typically those that have been in my programs awhile, will take on the role of a team-family big brother or big sister and monitor the emotional pulse of those around them.

A few years ago I came across a young woman participating on a local modified track team. I was not coaching her at the time, but in conversation, I gave her suggestions as to what would make her a better runner. At the time, she was often in trouble at school and spent a lot of time in the Dean's office, which didn't help her chances of remaining on the team. It was obvious to me she didn't believe in herself. One day, I asked her my infamous question "Where do you think you are on a scale of 1 to 10?" This young lady replied she was a 5 across the board. That's all I needed to hear. I knew with that response she didn't really believe in herself or her talent. As I got to know her, I found she had a lot of great qualities. They were just overpowered by the thicker insecure layers of that onion. She was acting as she thought she should to remain on the track team rather than showing her true colors, which, in this case, were her asset.

I took her under my wing for the next few years, and the day she finally won a race, she cried. She realized what she could accomplish if she were serious about her training. But the story doesn't end there. I told her, more than once, the footwear she wears outside of practice makes a difference. In my training program a runner should never wear flip flops—ever. I repeatedly remind athletes that support and care of their feet is critical. But she loved her flip flops. It was frustrating for me, but I remained on a mission. One day I pulled up to where she was working. I was stopping in to check out her feet, prepared to make a somewhat satirical comment about those flimsy rubber sandals. She smiled as I approached, and proudly displayed her proper footwear. Mission accomplished. She went on to break her school's record, at East Carolina University, and won a collegiate championship in the heptathlon. A heptathlon is a combined track and field event which requires an athlete (also known as a hep-tathlete) to participate in seven events, which include: 100-meter hurdle, high jump, shot put, 200-meter, long jump, javelin throw and 800-meter. I never give up on a kid. They need to know you really care.

THE MOTIVATIONAL T-SHIRT

I recently created a graphic for a new T-shirt that will be circulated to the athletes I work with. My puzzle design, at first glance, may appear similar to other promotional illustrations, but the message differs. The mantra, meant to embody inspiration, motivation and purpose, reads:

> *When the pieces are connected,*
> *you will experience success.*

As with the hundreds, maybe thousands, of T-shirts other young athletes wear to convey the essence of their team, this T-shirt is a tangible statement of my foundational message: The importance of syncing your mind, body and spirit. The significance of this message reaches well beyond the playing field and athletics. It's about developing into a person of reputable character, who has a sense of integrity and a great work ethic. It's about being a contributing member of your community, a loyal family member and a devoted person of faith. The message is about life lessons that, if synchronized at a young age, will sustain you for the long-term.

A lot of kids don't understand the commitment of real work and undeniable effort. They want to be the best without true commitment. Their young egos shout "You won't break me." I have a saying, "If you play with lousy people, you will remain lousy." But lousy isn't just related to skill ability, it's about attitude and effort. Fortunately it's a way of thinking that can be changed.

Steve D'Annunzio, Mission Driven Advisor and founder of the Soul Purpose Group, writes about meaningful effort. He states, "Build your life upon those efforts and resulting accomplishments that express the true beauty of who you are." He goes on to say, "The time you invest in meaningful effort will produce rewards that continue to grow more valuable."

For meaningful effort to occur in young athletes they need structure and guidance. It is a process that involves time. The completed puzzle will be a whole person in sync with their mind, body and spirit, not a group of fragmented mismatched pieces.

I look to develop respectable character in young people early on in the training process. Great things may come to unseasoned athletes, but it can easily be taken away. Talent can disappear, if not paired with good character. I tell my athletes to surround themselves with positive people, know individuals for who they are, get a good education, and don't wait for something bad to happen in your life before you begin praying. After all, as Dr. Ralph Martin states: "Prayer is, at root, simply paying attention to God."

FOCUS, WORK HARD, LEARN HOW TO SWEAT

Discovering an athlete's current level of strength, endurance and overall conditioning status can bring about a variety of responses from both parents and kids. Moms and dads will adamantly report their child is in great shape, with superior skills, and kids will rate themselves as an 8, if not higher, on a 1-to-10 scale. Their perceptions may or may not be accurate, but more often than not, my idea of being in shape is very different than theirs. For this reason I request that parents stay and observe the physical assessments I administer to their child. I want them to observe the results for themselves.

In defense of the parents, current perceptions of their child's skill may be distorted, for a number of reasons. They may not have been educated on proper strength and conditioning protocols, or were remiss in believing that training at a great facility, or purchasing the most expensive equipment will automatically produce a great athlete. Parents may have inadvertently guided their child to a feeling of entitlement, or allowed them to be less accountable for their actions than they should be. Bottom line, it's not about the facility or the field, it's about how an athlete is trained. Quite honestly, a substandard facility, with used equipment, can pump out great athletes—if those athletes have the desire to be a 10. Do you need a million-dollar weight room, or will a field of dreams suffice? Great facilities are nice, don't get me wrong, but it's not so much about the content as it is about an athlete's drive and what a trainer is capable of bringing out in them. Playing a sport doesn't necessarily mean you are training for that sport. And the results obtained with short-term training and conditioning will differ immensely from a program with long-term goals.

The preliminary physical evaluation I administer typically involves strength and endurance. Athletes are asked to run at various speeds, for a varying number of minutes, within a 15-minute time span. This exercise may take place on a field, in a gym, on a treadmill or possibly an elliptical. It may seem ordinary enough, but the actual test is difficult. From an athlete's end result, I can begin to form an idea of an athlete's current capabilities and what they have, versus what they need. Many kids will break and say they can't finish, but I look at them and they keep moving. I believe in all kids, but they have to believe in themselves.

USING MUSIC IN TRAINING

Kids will say "I can't jump rope anymore. I tried my best." I tell them "Put into your head the simple beat, one-two, one-two. The rhythm will give you more." And it does. One assumption we can all agree on, is that any music or rhythmic beat that motivates you will make you move more. Common sense suggests a faster beat will inspire the body to move faster. Music makes the time you are working out pass quickly, especially if the music is personally motivating and stimulating. Whether a cardio workout or strength training with weights, the type of music you chose can also enhance the intensity with which you work, and the duration of time you will remain physically engaged. I often recommend the use of classical music during training. For instance, Beethoven's fourth symphony—with over 140 beats per minute—is a good choice when you're trying to reach a higher impact in speed, strength and endurance. But classical music can also help relax the body. Non-lyrical, soothing music with a slower beat per measure can reduce blood pressure, heart rate and muscle tension. Neuroscientist Jack Lewis submits that "relaxing music has been shown to lower levels of cortisol in the body, the hormone associated with stress." Bottom line, if you would like to take a vacation from pop hits, hip hop, club, or dance music, try composers like Mozart, Beethoven, Bach, Verdi and Tchaikovsky during a strength and conditioning work out. Expand your knowledge base on the benefits of using classical music as it applies to your programming needs. On a scale of 1 to 10, the end result, as my athletes would say, is a 10.

> *Performance is more than just having talent.*
> *It's about drive, desire and determination*
> *to settle for nothing less than a ten.*

So where do the motivators that drive ambition, desire and determination come from? Can one really measure motivation? In his book, *Drive: The Surprising Truth About What Motivates Us*, Daniel Pink writes "If people don't know why they're doing what they're doing, how can you expect them to be motivated to do it." It relates back to my *Circle of Why* and defining purpose. Material compensation for a job well done, particularly early on in an athlete's career, rarely has long-term value. Undeniably, kids love to receive a trophy or other trinket recognizing an accomplishment, but so often these extrinsic rewards are based on an accomplishment that may not have been that great. Showing up for every game doesn't necessarily indicate drive, desire and determination. Kids often get away with saying they tried their hardest, or did their best, when they really didn't. A coach may say, "It doesn't matter if we lost, you tried your best!" and if they truly did try their best, that is fine. But what if they didn't? Extrinsic reinforcers, in these cases, are inappropriate messages an impressionable adolescent may carry through life.

> *I will instruct you and teach you*
> *in the way you should go;*
> *I will counsel you with my eye upon you.*
> —PSALM 32:8

A foundational principal in my synchronization process is identifying and developing intrinsic motivators. Though you can't really measure motivation, or the lack of motivation, as a trainer who knows your athletes, you should be able to recognize a person who has authentic determination. *The ability to develop or maintain a desire from within is what will truly motivate a young person to sustain the long journey necessary to become a premiere athlete.* As Daniel Pink says, "In environments where extrinsic rewards are most salient, many people work only to the point that triggers the reward—and no further." This performance is a 2 out of 10, at best. Pink goes on to state, "However, when contingent rewards aren't involved, or when incentives are used with the proper deftness, performance improves and understanding deepens... Meaningful achievement depends on lifting one's sights and pushing toward the horizon." His analogy of instructional motivation utilizing a carrots-and-sticks model suggests that amongst other things, this model can: extinguish intrinsic motivation, diminish performance, crowd out good behavior, encourage cheating, shortcuts and unethical behavior, become addictive and foster short-term thinking. Athletes need to set goals that promote competition with both themselves and others. A coach needs to be inherently curious. An individual's true potential will be more readily revealed if motivators are put in place to reach goals that have personal meaning and stimulate a person to explore, discover, learn, realize, understand and ultimately attain his or her authentic capability.

A person's level of faith also tends to play a role in identifying whether someone will be driven more by intrinsic or extrinsic motivators. Is the athlete driven to succeed by devotion and purpose, or the excessive need for possessions? Extrinsic rewards in professional sports are a carrot, no doubt. Look at the paychecks of professional athletes. But if young athletes can be inspired by intrinsic values and are taught the real priorities in life, they will remain grounded when they reach the level of premiere athlete and are faced with those extrinsic motivators and rewards (carrots).

> *Repetition of the same thought or*
> *physical action develops into a habit which,*
> *when repeated frequently enough,*
> *becomes an automatic reflex.*
> —NORMAN VINCENT PEALE,
> THE POWER OF POSITIVE THINKING

As a young athlete enters in the world of sports and ascends through the ranks, it will become apparent that many coaches care about every player, and some just want the great athlete, the stud. Even with young players, coaches are very often interested only in talent. They have a win-at-any-cost mentality. Control, a need to be in the limelight, jealousy, rivalry—there are many reasons people act the way they do. As a trainer and coach, my philosophy is kids first. I will give every young athlete a chance, and try my best to make every kid on a team an equal. Taking on an athlete who has little talent, no coordination and no belief in themselves, and flipping them in to something special is the sign of a good trainer.

Whoever restrains his words has knowledge,
and he who has a cool spirit
is a man of understanding."
—PROVERBS 17:2

For many coaches and trainers, staying inside the play-book box, is traditional and comfortable. Learning to sync a player's body is thinking outside of the box and coaches are often uncomfortable with this non-conforming aspect. Being a good coach isn't about being the loudest or most aggressive. Yelling at a child, often perceived as a motivator for results, doesn't typically work. It is about instruction of the mind, body and spirit. Somehow, somewhere, a correlation between success and how loud one can yell has been conceived, and many parents don't understand the mind, body and spirit concept. Do coaches that yell a lot win games? On occasion, but are those loud rants a detriment or benefit to players? Yelling to make a point is not a sustainable and effective strategy for attaining long-term goals. The need to win often becomes greater than allegiance to a moral code, or good character. Encourage players, inspire players, push them to their limits, but don't humiliate, bully or embarrass them. Feel the need to yell or intimidate? Turn to prayer rather than raise your temper in front of young impressionable minds.

WHEN YOU FALL YOU GET BACK ON YOUR FEET

A few years back I had a young woman starting out on my track team who was taking part in a conditioning workout that involved wall sits. This involves holding a chair-like position while leaning against a wall for a certain length of time. She kept falling and, when I approached her, she said she had given it all she could and couldn't do it anymore. I know the signs of muscle fatigue and her body wasn't there yet. I said to her "The next time you fall, everyone on the team will have to do ten more." She started crying, but she did it. After practice she told me, like I have heard so many times before, "I didn't believe in myself. I had no idea I would be able to do this. You pushed me. You train like we're a guy." No, I train like you're an athlete. Make it happen.

When the going gets tough, I tell my athletes to repeat "I will." Repeat those words over and over until your current mission is accomplished. In competition, it will be critical to never show your opponents you are tired. Coaches on the sidelines are looking for signs of fatigue.

> *There is real magic in enthusiasm.*
> *It spells the difference between mediocrity*
> *and accomplishment.*
> —*NORMAN VINCENT PEALE,*
> *AMERICAN MINISTER AND AUTHOR*

If you are a young athlete reading this, where do you think you are you on a scale of 1 to 10? Where are your priorities, your motivation, your drive, desire and determination? If you are a coach, or want to become a coach, ask yourself how you plan to help each athlete on your team focus and develop his or her strengths. Whether you're a coach or a player, put forth the effort to sync your mind, body and spirit and settle for nothing less than a 10.

CHAPTER FIVE

Roller-coaster ride
to success

I FIRST MET CHELSEA DUNAY early in the summer of 2004. She was attending a summer soccer camp where I was conducting the strength and conditioning training. Chelsea had decided to take on the goalie position and, as the expression goes, she was "all in." As a young teen going in to the seventh grade she trained like a high-school age athlete with a mission. She was a sponge, absorbing every morsel of information I offered, and her vision was very clear. Chelsea was motivated by the notion of being a great goalie—the best she could possibly be. She was the young athlete coaches dream of working with. A reserved, quick thinking, well coordinated adolescent wrapped in gritty, tough skin, Chelsea was the textbook persona for what would be an up-and-coming NCAA All-American Athlete.

My introduction to the athletes at the camp was not unlike the first day at other camps I have run. I explained the necessity of developing a strong foundation. We would assess each persons starting point and begin the building process. Then, unfortunately for some, the reality check would take place. I would find out who was in shape and who wasn't; who was at camp to actually work out and who came thinking this would be a good way to bump off part of their day; who really had a good mindset. Though Chelsea wouldn't come close to a synced 10 on my mind, body and spirit scale for some time, she was driven. As family is the top priority for all the athletes I work with, it was only a matter of time before I found out just how driven Chelsea and the rest of the Dunay household really were. It is said adversity introduces a man to himself. In this case it was a family.

The summer of 2005 came along, and with it, another round of summer training camps. One camp I run is not dedicated to a particular sport, so each year there is a melting pot of participants. This session, Chelsea decided to bring her brother as he was rather inactive at the time. She felt he could stand to lose a few pounds. Her brother, Mitch, was a good-spirited young lad who would be entering the fourth grade. He had a fledgling interest in playing football or lacrosse but, was casually non-committal. He was there to focus on the goal his big sister had set for him—becoming more physically active. Mitch had a primary purpose, which was a great place to start. My strength and conditioning camps focused on getting ready for a variety of sports, so he was in the right place. Specialized skill development, specific to game play, would come with another coach at another time and another location.

Summer training camp melds many age groups and varying levels of talent together, but the individual goals and objectives remain personal. Each aspiring athlete needs to begin the developmental process from their current bedrock. As a returning athlete, Chelsea's base was going to be a bit different than her brother Mitch's would be, and that was okay. There was a four-year age difference between the two siblings and at this point, the less Mitch knew about what his physical regime was going to be, the better.

For an aspiring young athlete to develop the tools of longevity, their skill set must go beyond their potential physical prowess. A person must develop their mind and the ability to think logically, resourcefully and productively. A person must develop their ability to speak articulately and intelligibly. And a person must learn how to win, not how in the sense of having the superior score, but how in the manner in which you attain and acknowledge victory. Specifically: The proficient ability to act with humility.

CREATIVE THINKING

To expand on these concepts, my camps routinely take a few left turns on the road to game day. To focus on mental preparedness, the kids play a variety of brain fitness exercises, often referred to by the name Brain Gym®. These exercises stimulate the brain, promoting improvement and efficiency in concentration, memory, reflex, problem solving and creative thinking. These brain workouts all aid in the ability to be optimally prepared mentally for both training and game play. I also involve athletes in a session of skits, an adolescent version of dramatic play. I group the athletes randomly and pick a theme for the parodies, for example, the word Motown. From that point on there are just three simple rules to follow:

1 *Decide on a song, either a made-up original or an adapted version of an existing tune.*

2 *Create some type of physical move, like dancing, that the group will perform as a unit.*

3 *Perform the finished product in front of the entire camp.*

Teaching kids to be mindful, creative thinkers is a gift that will be used for a lifetime, whether they decide to pursue athletics or not. The tasks I present are motivating and fun for the youth, yet, as a group, there is so much more occurring. The kids are selecting and identifying information, applying and analyzing choices, synthesizing and evaluating the process and listening and interacting with each other—all while having a great time generating a finished product. The finished products never cease to amaze me. One year a group created a human tennis court, acting out a game where kids were the equipment, the sound effects and the players. Another group made a human car complete with the clatter-and-clank noises of an automobile in motion. One year, Chelsea's brother, Mitch, was involved with a group that acted out the grappling of two Sumo wrestlers. It was a youthful, light-hearted parody of a sport that originated in Japan. Each year the presentations are awesome, and the opportunity for young kids to utilize and expand their creative thinking skills in a meaningful forum, amongst their peers, is a delight to witness.

PUBLIC SPEAKING

With the avalanche of technology immersing a generation of children in a personal relationship with their smartphone, iPad or other high-tech device, the art of conversation seems to be somewhat buried in the snow. Texting a friend sitting two feet away, rather than striking up a face-to-face conversation, is no longer considered abnormal behavior. Exposing children to the opportunity to speak publicly and to openly converse with others has never been more important.

At summer camp, another event the youth take part in is referred to as center stage. Individually, athletes are asked to stand in front of the group. Often the initial experience is stressful and uncomfortable. Most participants have never spoken in front of a group before, and they don't know how to handle themselves. The current speaker is asked to address the audience on a topic they are somewhat familiar with, and then they must respond to the crowd during a question and answer period. Through this sequence, I encourage public speaking basics like good posture, making eye contact and not repeatedly saying *umm* or *ah*. These tools will have practical application throughout life. The increased confidence that comes with practice and improved public speaking skills will positively impact one's conduct on the playing field as well as possible media dialogue after a game, a job interview and many other situations. It's an opportunity for shy students to come out of their shell and likewise an opportunity to calm the nervousness most athletes experience when first speaking in front of others. Parents will routinely comment on the positivity and confidence they see in their child's demeanor following their participation in these activities. The ability to present one's self in conversation with self-assured ease is a tool that can be used throughout life in countless circumstances. Learning to think before you speak, knowing when to remain silent, and eliminating the word *um* from your vocabulary are all priceless lessons in public speaking.

Mitch and Chelsea, though physically hard at work, were both a bit shy when I first met them as young kids. Sessions like these helped prime their minds for all that was to come.

COMPETITION

Look up the word *competition*, and you will read definitions like: the activity or condition of competing, rivalry for supremacy, or a contest for some prize, honor, or advantage. Synonyms include words like challenge, opposition, battle, tournament and game. The word competition typically centers on the idea of beating another team or individual. With that focus comes the debate about the validity of competition and the experience of the sweet-smell-of-success. Is there a right way to compete, or a defining purpose for promoting participation in contests? Commenting in regard to Mitch, Chelsea, Breanna, Bryce and the other athletes I have written about in this book, as well as all the athletes I work with in training, the answer is yes, there is a purpose.

Competition can be against someone, or something, including against yourself. As I teach young athletes to sync their mind, body and spirit, learning to compete successfully is a necessity, not just on the playing field, but in life. The key is to keep your competitive spirit positive and constructive, free of destructive actions and disparaging remarks.

We have all heard the phrase "competition is the spice of life," and it's true. Regardless of what you choose to do with your life you will, at one time or another, be in the midst of some kind of competition. Competition teaches people how to work for results, whether it's an athletic competition, a job interview or competing against yourself, to attain a desired grade-point average, or fitness goal.

Without competition, we would all be average, and probably rather inactive under-achievers. Seeking to work collaboratively on a project is certainly a rational, and educated way to team up and pool resources to attain results. With that said, one also has to possess a certain level of competitive spirit to remain at the top of his or her game. People tend to work harder when there is a deadline or goal involved. We also learn from our mistakes. Though losing is often unfairly categorized as failure, regaining momentum after a failure can give us courage in all aspects of our lives. In these prime formative years, youth can be taught to cultivate healthy competition into everyday life. Learning to challenge themselves improves personal goals, and preparing to win, promotes innovation and creative thinking. It's about developing and syncing the whole package—that package is you.

Young athletes need to believe in themselves to remain competitive. To attain the ability to believe in one's self, consider the value of failure. Once an athlete has experienced, and recovered from failure, they understand they can indeed produce and succeed. It circles back to my scale of 1 to 10, assessing where are you now and where you want to be. As a team, the goal is to win. In becoming a premiere athlete, the competition becomes individualized and personal as well.

With Chelsea, Mitch and other athletes I have trained, nothing becomes more of an individualized competition than attaining the short-term goals that keep them moving up the scale, rather than stalling at a 5 or a 6. If the task is flipping oversized tires, then do it. If you're required to climb a fence that seems too difficult, climb it anyway. If the task is an intense two-minute sprint, then complete the task in two minutes, not less, not more, but two minutes. And give each challenge everything you have. Without a competitive spirit, when your body starts hurting, you will mentally stop competing. You have to train yourself to keep going. How you handle those minutes of pain can lead to a win or a loss. Whether it's the physical pain of an athletic endeavor, or another pain in life, you have to keep going. Leave the game at the same level and the same intensity at which you started. Remain driven and determined, with a purpose, and include the words *strong-willed* on the pages of your playbook for success.

> *A human life is a story told by God.*
> —HANS CHRISTIAN ANDERSON,
> DANISH AUTHOR

The summer of 2009, Chelsea would be entering the twelfth grade. She was entering her final season of soccer and, up to this point, her high school career had been very successful. Chelsea's goal was to be a collegiate soccer goalie, and her eyes were set on being a member of the Tribe, the athletic nickname for Division III, College of William & Mary. Mitch would be entering the eighth grade playing both modified lacrosse and football. Both siblings continued to attend my summer training programs, and I worked with the duo on strength and conditioning in the off-season, as well. But, their pleasant well-mannered behavior was masking an abyss, of sorts. The family was quietly dealing with a circumstance whose name alone stops most people in their tracks—cancer. Chelsea and Mitch's mom had been diagnosed with brain cancer a few years earlier, but with an optimistic outlook, their lives carried on as normally as is possible in these situations.

Chelsea was off to the College of William & Mary in the fall of 2010. Playing goalie for the soccer team was a dream she desperately wanted. She had worked hard through high school to develop that sync in mind, body and spirit, and though she knew her continued journey would require an unquestionable commitment, she was ready for the challenge. There was just one final hurdle she had to clear before donning the goalkeeper gear: To be a member of the team she had to pass a fitness test. This prerequisite is not uncommon in college sports, but as a freshman, the process was still very nerve wracking. Chelsea passed the test and, with each new training season, that qualifying assessment became more of a technicality. Self-assured conviction had replaced sheer anxiety.

Mitch had his own dreams at that time. In 2009, he would be entering the ninth grade and his interest in football was becoming solidified. He had developed a timeline of sorts for himself, wanting to first play football at Penn State (pre-scandal) and then move on to the NFL. He had set his aspirations high and his dreams were a great motivational goal for him. In the meantime, their mother continued her valiant fight to overcome brain cancer. Each of their goals, both personal and as a family, was fuel for their journey.

> *The difficulties of life are intended*
> *to make us better, not bitter.*
> —*AUTHOR UNKNOWN*

Chelsea continued to train with me when she was not away at school. Our goal was for her to remain fit, and physically prepared. As a college senior, her patience and determination paid off. She would begin the season as the starting goalie.

Mitch and Chelsea had attended summer training camp for years, but in the summer of 2009, I saw that age and maturity had produced a dramatic change in Mitch's athletic profile. I could see that underneath the skin of his maturing body was a linebacker waiting to burst out. My own coaching schedule, and the training protocols for the football team, left our conditioning time together to Mitch's off-season. This obstacle was limiting his full potential but, believing all things happen for a reason, we trained as often and as hard as we could during that time.

Mitch had some playing time during those years but his talent was mired down. In 2013, that all changed. That year, I was able to roll our off-season training into football season, and the results, from the perspective of his strength and endurance capabilities, were incredible. Offensively, Mitch led his high school team with 1,313 yards rushing and 19 touchdowns. His defensive play was equally impressive with 150 tackles. Mitch was reaping the benefits of hard work and began to really see himself playing on a college football team. But in this dream, it was no longer Penn State. Though a pipe dream, at best, he had developed his own college playbook, and one of the schools on his roster was Princeton. Princeton, the fourth-oldest university in the United States, an Ivy League legacy with alumni that include U.S. presidents, Supreme Court justices, scholars and the like. His play his senior year had given him some exposure to college recruiters, including one close to home, Syracuse University. But Princeton? Could he do it and would he do it? Only time would tell.

> *A bend in the road is not the end of the road...*
> *unless you fail to make the turn.*
> —AUTHOR UNKNOWN

Mitch's highly successful football season ended with well-deserved fanfare, but his mother's cancer was not giving the family reason to celebrate, as they had hoped. This dreadful disease was spreading. She had attended all but one game, when she was recovering from surgery, but she was losing mobility and the prognosis was not good. Mitch remained stoic and, though aware of what was becoming inevitable, he spoke very little about what was to be. His time with his mother was in the present.

While Mitch was finishing up his stellar football season, Chelsea was in the midst of her own incredible experience. Her soccer team had made it through the play-offs and was heading to San Antonio, Texas for the NCAA Division III National Championships. It was only the second time in history this soccer team had made it to the finals, and the first time at the big game in over 20 years. Since Chelsea had first told me she wanted to study medicine in college, I began calling her Doc. That is the only name I now use to refer to her. She called me before the team left for Texas, and my words to her were simple. A few words put into perspective the years of work syncing her mind, body and spirit, developing the confident ability to handle the pressure of goalkeeper in a national championship game: "Go win the championship, Doc."

Mitch and his parents were traveling to the game as well. His mother's health continued to deteriorate, but with three determined minds she would be able to make the trip to watch Chelsea play. William & Mary won the National Championship with a 2-0 win over Trinity College. Chelsea made nine saves, and earned all-tournament honors. Those accolades would be on top of her All-American status, and other awards accumulated in her tenure on the team. Her dream had become a reality, and her mom was able to witness it all.

> *When life gives you a hundred reasons to cry,*
> *Show life that you have a thousand reasons to smile".*
> —AUTHOR UNKNOWN

As Chelsea secured a soccer championship and Mitch completed a successful high school varsity football season, Mitch was finding himself in a tackle play, of sorts, off the field. Only this situation had an academic yellow flag, and no officials to argue the call with. The ACT, American College Testing, is a standardized college entrance exam. The exam is offered on several dates, and in numerous locations across each state, throughout the summer and fall of a student's senior year. The scores on this test are an important consideration in the college admission process. By this time, Mitch had narrowed down his college choices and, with his father's encouragement, Princeton was now at the top of his list. He had taken the ACT and received his results. Unfortunately, in December of that year, after a third try, Mitch received a disappointing setback. He had scored a 26. To be accepted into his Ivy League dream school, he needed a score of 27. As a potential incoming athlete, there were a limited number of openings available to accommodate Mitch's situation. But he would need to score that one more point. With the encouragement of Princeton coaches, and a will to succeed, Mitch signed up to take the test one last time. The only problem with this registration was that in February he would have to travel out of state. New York had no testing sites scheduled for that month so he would hit the road to the closest available testing site, which was Wilkes-Barre, Pennsylvania, about a three-hour drive.

Through all of this, the health of Mitch and Chelsea's mom was deteriorating rapidly. Cancer had taken its toll and each day became more precious. In this time his mom had also had a dream. It was a premonition she shared with Mitch shortly before his official visit to Princeton. In her vision, Mitch attended the Ivy League. Then, on January 24, 2014, Mitch and Chelsea's beloved mom passed away. An angel on earth was now in the eternal hands of God.

The ACT tests were in two weeks and Mitch had a full plate of activity. He chose to continue as his mother would have insisted, and kept his schedule tight. He studied as hard as he could and prepared himself mentally and spiritually for the exam. He was as prepared for this exam as he could possibly be, but whether he could achieve the score he needed was still to be determined. The days ticked by after he took the test, as it would be a couple of weeks before the scores were sent electronically. The day finally arrived and Mitch did an early-morning check on his computer. No results were posted, but Mitch would check again during his first opportunity at school. On the next check, the tag he was waiting for appeared.

With the help of a friend to make the initial glance, Mitch would hear a number he had hoped and prayed for. A number he had worked so hard for and overcome so many obstacles to attain—the number 28. He would be going to Princeton.

> *Failure is the condiment*
> *that gives success its flavor.*
> —TRUMAN CAPOTE, AUTHOR, SCREENWRITER,
> PLAYWRIGHT AND ACTOR

In the fall of 2014, Mitch arrived at Princeton. His dream was now a reality. What started as a fantasy had become a reality. In the last few years Mitch had been dealt the type of adversity that would have led others to throw in the towel. With a purpose and the determination to reach the goals he had set for himself, Mitch continued to clear every obstacle placed in his path. With a supportive father as his number one fan, a caring sister encouraging him, and the divine presence of his mother's smile looking at him with angelic and unadulterated pride, Mitch walked on to the football field at Princeton University donning the number 45.

For his first season as a Tiger, Mitch played running-back and full-back positions. He had a successful year, but Mitch knows his future playing potential is completely in his hands. On that scale of 1 to 10 he has a few more numbers to conquer, and he knows it. But he's prepared to continue the synchronization process. I still talk with Mitch once or twice a week on the phone, and he will continue to train with me when he is home on college vacations. To hold his current position on the Tiger team, Mitch knows he has to work his body physically, mentally and spiritually. There are no handouts in Division I college football. Establishing longevity will be key. As for his dream of becoming a professional football player, I like to think it's not if, but when. Mitch and Chelsea have endured a roller-coaster ride to athletic success. Chelsea has accomplished her athletic goal and shifted her purpose from premiere athlete, to M.D. As for Mitch, well, his dream is still alive. Besides, we have a bet. I'm extremely afraid of heights, but I have promised Mitch I will step outside of my comfort zone the day I hear he has made it into the NFL. I will ride the roller coaster of his choice anywhere in the United States. I just hope this coaster doesn't bear the name Kingda Ka, Iron Rattler or Wicked Twister!

CHAPTER SIX

Willpower & the need for speed

WHEN YOU HEAR OR THINK of the word willpower, descriptors that come to mind include words like determination, self-control, drive and self-discipline. When I hear the word willpower, I often envision an athlete I have been working with for several years now. I see an athlete who runs with the same intense speed on land as the fastest animal on the planet, the peregrine falcon, displays in flight; an athlete who displays grace and humility both on and off the football field; an athlete who has achieved that unsurpassable number 10 on my scale to success, yet remains very aware of what he must do to maintain that status; an athlete whose name is synonymous with athletic proficiency at its finest; an athlete who has learned to sync his mind, body and spirit, and to reap the rewards of hard work and steadfast motivation. His name is familiar to fans of the national football league, and his record breaking statistics speak for themselves. His name is Tyvon Branch. Tyvon began his professional career as a safety for the NFL Oakland Raiders. He will begin the 2015 training season playing for the AFC West Kansas City Chiefs.

On July 14, 2012, Branch signed a four-year, 26.6 million dollar contract with the Raiders—impressive, to say the least. But like any sport, change is often inevitable. He recently signed a new deal with the Chiefs. But there is something that drives Tyvon more than the money. Something that inspires him to remain committed to his goal, in spite of the rigors of long-term training. It's something that has clear purpose, and its given Tyvon the determined willpower to persevere and to become the greatest athlete he has the God-given potential to become. That something is his legacy.

> *The difference between a successful person*
> *and others is not a lack of strength,*
> *not a lack of knowledge, but rather a lack of will.*
> —VINCENT LOMBARDI,
> LEGENDARY FOOTBALL COACH

At a time when highly paid athletes sometimes appear disconnected from, or disinterested in, the fans, or use their fame and fortune to conduct themselves in a way that screams arrogance, superiority and narcissism, Tyvon remains spiritually balanced and humble. Looking back several years, though, this wasn't always the case. Physically, with the exception of a few unforeseen injuries, he has demonstrated nothing but talent since high school. The essence of his mind and spirit, however, weren't always as polished. It wouldn't be until after Tyvon's initiation into the NFL that I received a phone call. The rest would be history.

I first saw Tyvon in action in the fall of 2001. He entered Cicero North Syracuse High School, a suburban district a few miles north of Syracuse, as a sophomore after transferring from an urban school. One of nine children, word of his physical talent preceded his arrival. Tyvon's previous coaches, as well as those who had already seen him compete, were circulating word of his superior talent. To say he was fast was an understatement. On the football field at his new school, Tyvon was the standout varsity player. He earned second-team All-State, All-Central New York and All-Area honors as a tailback and outside linebacker. I was coaching modified football at the time and, though I knew who he was and was aware of his talent, I really had no direct contact with him. His cousin, Artie, was a player on my team and I heard bits and pieces of his happenings, but our worlds had not yet overlapped.

In addition to football, Tyvon was on the indoor and outdoor track and field teams. It was on the track during his senior year that I got a good look at him in action. He was good, really good. Coach Dowdell—my girls' indoor and outdoor track and field assistant—and I starting putting in some extra training time with him after regular practice. It was nothing intense, just some additional guidance. Tyvon was in the capable hands of a veteran boys' coach.

In early spring of his senior year, I traveled to New York City with a few of the girls on my track team who had qualified for the Indoor National Championships. Tyvon had qualified as well, and would be competing in the 60-meter and 200-meter run. On March 14, 2004, Tyvon won the National Indoor Track Championship in the 60-meter with a time of 6.82 seconds. He also posted a personal best in the 200-meter race. He would go on to be named the 2004 Gatorade New York State Track Athlete of the Year. Tyvon set a school record as well and would finish first in the state in both the 100- and 200-meter. He was an athletic prodigy, of sorts. As I silently watched Tyvon, it was clear to me that he was, undeniably, talented—but I had seen great talent before. Whether he had developed his mind and spirit as well as his body, creating a synced path to longevity, only time would tell.

> *Talent is God-given. Be humble.*
> *Fame is man-given. Be grateful.*
> *Conceit is self-given. Be careful.*
> —JOHN WOODEN,
>   LEGENDARY UCLA HEAD BASKETBALL COACH

Tyvon went on to play four years of football at the University of Connecticut. His successes in high school had made for a seamless transition to his position on the football team. Tyvon had a strong, lean physique powered by incredible speed. He continued to amass mind-boggling statistics and was a force to be reckoned with on both offense and defense. As a junior, Tyvon was regarded as the fastest cornerback in college football. He was maturing, and considered a leader and a mentor to younger players on the team. In 48 games at Connecticut, Tyvon started in 31. Football success had been sweet and as the door to college play closed, the door to the NFL seemed to be cracking open.

But with every future, comes a past. Tyvon was no different and had left some proverbial skeletons behind in his UCONN closet. In 2005, Tyvon had been arrested with five other Connecticut players after an incident involving another motor vehicle. He was released after posting bail and the matter was eventually reconciled. Academics, or more likely an apathy or indifference to class work, had been a problem for Tyvon. His focus was on game tapes and football strategies. And, up to this point, that formula for success on the football field had worked. Tyvon had also become comfortable relying on his God-given talent and hadn't spent the time he needed to in the weight room. He was savoring the present as, in his eyes, his future seemed to be unfolding like a perfectly played touchdown return. Through those four years, I followed Tyvon's college career and kept in touch with Tyvon's cousin, Artie. Artie was hoping our paths would cross, but for now it wasn't in the plan.

There would be several big days leading up to the NFL draft. The biggest asset Tyvon had going for him was speed. At the 2008 NFL Scouting Combine, Tyvon ran a 4.31 second 40-yard dash. He was drafted by the Oakland Raiders in the fourth round, one hundredth overall. Tyvon Branch was living his dream. He was now a professional football player.

Setting a goal is not the main thing.
It is deciding how you will go about achieving it
and staying with that plan.
      —TOM LANDRY,
         LEGENDARY FOOTBALL COACH AND PLAYER

Artie was one of Tyvon's greatest supporters, and though he wished success for his cousin, he could read between the blurred lines. After a tumultuous, but acceptable, rookie year in the NFL, Tyvon needed to get his act together. He could not survive by sheer talent alone and if he didn't become more disciplined, his talent would start to have a tumbledown effect. He could easily become another statistic, gobbled up by the shock and awe of the NFL.

In the summer of 2009, I received a phone call. It was from Artie, who was calling on behalf of Tyvon. Tyvon, he said, would begin to train with me immediately. The days of living on past accolades and physical prowess were just that—history. If Tyvon truly wanted to be an NFL player of merit and distinction, with long-term viability, he did indeed need to get his act together. The first stop: A visit to the reservoir.

I look at all people equally. I'm not a star-personality gawker. I was certainly aware of Tyvon's accomplishments. But, being a professional athlete didn't make him an automatic scholar in all things football, particularly when it came to strength and conditioning. I needed to discover who Tyvon really was and where he was on my scale of 1 to 10. Yes, his talent seemed an unquestionable 10, but how was that talent synced to his mental preparedness, goals and purpose? I was about to find out.

Without self-discipline, success is impossible, period.
      —LOU HOLTZ, COLLEGE FOOTBALL ANALYST
         FOR ESPN AND FORMER FOOTBALL COACH

Tyvon ran the reservoir under the same requirements as other athletes I take there—sprint up the 700' incline in 45 seconds, or fewer, with a two-minute maximum allotted to descend the slope, regroup, and repeat the task. He did it, but with less than impressive results, for me anyway. He would be back again and again and again until his struggle to complete the rounds became motivation to continue. He would be back until the stumbling blocks and justifications turned to determination, and until his lifeblood was one of humility. If Tyvon wanted longevity, he needed a plan and a purpose—a soul purpose. He needed a cause. He needed the inspiration to sync his mind and spirit, as well as his body, to develop the self-motivation necessary to become the greatest football player he had the potential to be.

Steve D'Annunzio, author of the book *The Prosperity Paradigm* describes soul purpose this way: "Soul Purpose is your unique series of talents, strengths, passions, interests, hobbies, attitudes, and values that form the essence of the most magnificent version of you." He goes on to describe cause as the guiding beacon whenever fear, doubt, and worry assail you. It guides you to have faith, and the will to persist in times of challenge.

Tyvon needed to return to the Oakland Raiders in 2009 as a self-motivated man of confidence, a man with a cause, a man with a mission uniquely his own. He came to me with a commitment to achieve and I, in return, made the same commitment.

> *The Law of Responsibility—I am 100%*
> *responsible for every aspect of my life.*
> —STEVE D'ANNUNZIO,
> THE PROSPERITY PARADIGM

As we started his strength and conditioning program, Tyvon considered bulking up a bit by adding a few pounds to his frame. The extra weight could potentially enhance his defensive skills. It could also compromise his speed. The strategy would not be in weight gain, but in training. The ideal weight for Tyvon was, and still is, around 205 pounds. He had regularly scheduled workouts and on more than one occasion I combined his workout sessions with another athlete I was training, basketball phenom, Breanna Stewart.

The weight room was not Tyvon's favorite place. In the past he had done the training regimes he was required to do, but that was about it. He lacked willpower, and he knew it. To exacerbate the problem, when using weights, Tyvon's grip was slightly compromised, the result of broken fingers, a common injury in this sport. In the past, Tyvon had wrapped his hands for support but that was a routine I wanted to discontinue. He was told to no longer wear the wraps. He wore them anyway. NFL player or not, gifted talent or not, that would be the last time Tyvon would disrespect my training protocol. It would also be the last time he had to complete a rigorous work out twice in one session. A commitment to my training program meant there were rules to be followed. All in.

On one of our trips to the reservoir, Tyvon decided to bring along a friend, a fellow professional football player he occasionally worked out with. Darius Butler, a cornerback for the Indianapolis Colts, arrived ready to run. This pint-sized mountain certainly didn't appear as challenging to Darius as Tyvon had made it out to be when describing his workout sessions here. After all, how difficult could it be to run up and downhill three or four times? The guidelines for completion were reviewed and the two buff athletes began the ascent. Darius ran a couple of laps and his hamstrings called it quits. As the saying goes, he was ready to eat crow. The luscious green knoll that masked a torturous workout had fooled him. With a smile on his face, Darius tweeted, "Pete is the craziest guy I've ever met. I never want to train with him again." Tyvon looked at him and said, "Welcome to my world." I said not a word, but smiled as we walked back to the car.

> *Today I will do what others won't,*
> *so tomorrow I can accomplish what others can't.*
> —*Jerry Rice*,
> *Hall of Fame Football Wide Receiver*

Tyvon returned for the 2009 season as the starting strong safety. He would go on to start in all 16 games that season finishing with 98 unassisted tackles and 26 assists, 2 forced fumbles, and a sack. For Tyvon, the win was now from within. It was more than physical prowess but a sync of mind, body and spirit. Tyvon now understood the significance of having authentic purpose and what it takes to establish longevity.

In the 2010 season Tyvon again started all 16 games for the Oakland Raiders. And in March of 2012 came the franchise tag. In the course of the next few seasons various athletic injuries cut into his playing time. In September of 2014 Tyvon broke the fifth metatarcel in his foot and required surgery. He was placed on injured reserve and was out for the rest of the season. Though obviously disappointing, Tyvon remained optimistic about his recovery.

In March of 2015 Tyvon was let go by the Oakland Raiders. Later that same month he was signed on by the Kansas City Chiefs. Tyvon is synced and ready to play. As long as he remains injury free, his skills on the field remain exceptional. The reality of changeover in the NFL is no surprise. Tyvon continues to pay it forward by giving back to his community. He visits schools regularly and is involved in several organizations including the Central New York Football Academy, United Way and the NFL Play 60 Campaign. In 2015 Tyvon will begin his eighth season in the NFL.

The stepping stones from high school champion, to college star and then professional athlete haven't come without adversity, but that's okay. It's those moments of difficulty that help define our character, challenge our resilience and determine just how motivated we really are in reaching a goal—valuable lessons in life. What we do with those lessons will be completely up to us. How do you want to be remembered? Tyvon wants a legacy. Will it be in football? In business? In community service? God's plan is still unfolding, but one guarantee is that I will be there for him every step of the way.

CHAPTER SEVEN

There's no such thing as a former Marine

PRIDE, INTEGRITY AND HONOR are intangible qualities many people seek. A lesser number of people actually commit to exhibiting these character traits for even a short period of time, much less a sustained period of their adult life. One need only look in the direction of a Marine to see someone who has chosen to exhibit these character traits, as well as determination, purpose and drive.

Kyle Francis is a brother in this *semper-fidelis* family but, at 26 years of age, he is no longer on active duty. The bloodied uniform he was wearing May 13, 2010, the day of a Taliban ambush in Afghanistan, hangs humbly in his living room. The memory of what he survived is a daily inspiration, and a silent reminder of the friends who didn't make it. He is forever faithful. Proudly trained in a culture that demands excellence and loyalty,

Kyle is now using his motivational skills to work with me, as well as others, trading a battlefield for an athletic field.

Kyle doesn't like to be referred to as a hero. Even with a Purple Heart for wounds he received in combat, and a Bronze Star for heroism—just two of thirteen metals he received on his tour of duty—the word *hero* makes him uncomfortable. He considers those who didn't return to be the real heroes. Kyle instead focuses his time on what he now considers his life purpose: Training aspiring young athletes to become the best that they can be.

> *The two most important days in your life are the*
> *day you were born and the day you find out why.*
> —MARK TWAIN,
> AMERICAN AUTHOR AND HUMORIST

Kyle's presence alone speaks volumes about who he is and what he stands for. His perseverance reaches deeper than the average person could begin to imagine. He is tough—and stubborn. The word, quit, is not in his vocabulary. Kyle doesn't talk much at all about what he has endured these last few years, but in my eyes, Kyle is a hero, a champion, a conqueror. His story needs to be told.

Kyle graduated from high school in 2006. He initially went to work for a local company, but in 2008 decided to enter the military. With an athletic body and a good head on his shoulders, he was a recruiter's dream. Kyle had his own dream as well. He wanted to become a Marine. The first stop in the process of becoming a Marine is the Marine Corps Recruit Depot in San Diego, California. It is there that paperwork is filled out, documents are signed and you officially become a recruit. Kyle lived east of the Mississippi, so after his short stopover at the Depot, he continued on to Parris Island, South Carolina. His journey had begun.

I coached Kyle in football, and he participated in my strength and training programs over the years, but after graduation our paths would cross with less frequency. Kyle survived training camp and loved being a Marine. He planned on making military service his career, but he also knew the risks. A Marine looks danger in the eye and doesn't blink. He would fear nothing.

In May of 2010, Kyle was on assignment, stationed in Afghanistan. He was caught in a Taliban ambush, and sustained two bullet wounds to his left leg and one through his right hand. His leg wounds were very serious, but he would survive. Two of his comrades, just inches to his right, would not. Kyle required emergency surgery immediately following the incident. He was medivacked to Landstuhl Regional Medical Center, in Germany, by way of nearby Ramstein Air Base. Landstuhl serves as the nearest treatment center for wounded soldiers coming from Iraq and Afghanistan, as well as the stop-over medical facility for seriously injured soldiers before they're flown on to the United States. When Kyle was stable enough for additional travel, he came back to the states for further medical treatment and rehabilitation at the National Naval Medical Center in Bethesda, Maryland, a sprawling campus now more commonly referred to as the Walter Reed National Military Medical Center. His plan as a brave, strong and fearless 22-year-old, was to return to active duty as soon as possible. Kyle's nine-month recuperation was long and painful. Seventy-two days in the hospital, and several more excruciating operations, were combined with numerous road trips from central New York to Maryland for follow up appointments, and further medical treatments. Through it all, his family was there to help and support Kyle in any way they could.

Unable to go back on active duty, Kyle completed rehab and headed to Miami. He needed space. After Miami he spent some time in Connecticut, and then headed back to his family home in Clay, New York. Kyle's wounds were not healing as well or as quickly as he had hoped. He continued to wear a Taylor spatial frame, or external fixator, on his lower left leg. The fixator was a circular, metal frame with two rings that fit around his leg. The frame attached to his bone with pins that extended from the rings through the bone to the other side. These crosspieces could be independently lengthened or shortened, repositioning bones in the direction necessary for treatment. Kyle remained outwardly optimistic about his full recovery, but the idea of returning to active duty was becoming a blurred shade of gray. Kyle's parents, Lisa and Lamar, could see the signs of depression settling in. He was spending more and more time alone and sedentary. Only a fellow Marine could even begin to understand what Kyle had endured. And though others were willing to listen, Kyle wasn't necessarily willing to talk. Their persistent efforts to stimulate his spirits seemed futile—until another idea came to mind. They would call an old friend. Kyle's parents and I grew up together and, though we hadn't remained in close contact, they knew I still trained young athletes in the area.

The call I received came from the heart of loving and concerned parents. There was no hesitation in my response. I would do whatever was necessary to help Kyle persevere through this difficult time. Instinctively, Kyle had also recognized that to mentally and emotionally survive the curveball he had been thrown, he needed to re-sync himself. And that's exactly what he began to do.

I started driving Kyle to his physical therapy sessions. Following PT, he and I would continue with extended workout sessions at his home. Strenuous workouts seemed to be paying off, and, for the first time in months, he was able to walk a few steps without his crutches. Kyle joined me as my assistant at track and field practices, as well as strength and conditioning workouts. As time passed, Kyle retired from active duty. He had discovered a new purpose in life and his spirits were high.

> *A Marine is a Marine. ...there's no such thing*
> *as a former Marine. You're a Marine, just in*
> *a different uniform and you're in a different*
> *phase of your life. But you'll always be a Marine*
> *because you went to Parris Island, San Diego or*
> *the hills of Quantico. There's no such thing*
> *as a former Marine.*
>
> —GENERAL JAMES F. AMOS,
> 35TH COMMANDANT OF THE MARINE CORPS

In the fall of 2011, Kyle noticed he was losing strength in his hands and legs. His mother, Lisa, also noticed changes in her son's day-to-day abilities. Tasks he had been able to do were now becoming a bit of a challenge. The curve ball thrown into his journey had finally seemed to be straightening itself out, but the symptoms Kyle was experiencing could not be ignored.

On March 14, 2012, at the age of 24, Kyle was diagnosed with Amyotrophic Lateral Sclerosis (ALS). Kyle had Lou Gehrig's disease. The muscles of people with ALS grow progressively weaker, and eventually the disease causes paralysis. It's an incurable, fatal, neuromuscular disease. While others receiving this type of diagnosis may have changed their life's traffic light to stop, Kyle did just the opposite. He neither seeks, nor wants, a pity party from anyone. His life light is on green. He leaves a truly indescribable impact on young people that must be experienced first-hand to be understood. I love this man and everything he stands for. He is my motivation to become a better person.

For those of you who tuned in to the ESPY awards in July of 2014, and those of you who didn't, you've most likely heard segments of the poignant speech Stuart Scott, long time voice at SportsCenter, gave as he received the Jimmy V Perseverance Award. The award is named in memory of Jim Valvano, the famed North Carolina basketball coach who died of cancer in

1993. Scott, too, died of cancer in January of 2015, but not before sharing these powerful words: "When you die, that does not mean that you lose to cancer. You beat cancer by how you live, why you live, and the manner in which you live. So live. Live. Fight like hell." This is the path Kyle has chosen.

Your first perception of Kyle may be skewed, depending on where that first impression takes place. In public, Kyle speaks with a soft polite voice, and is even a bit reserved. Once in the weight room, or on the training field, the Marine in Kyle emerges. He shouts with enthusiasm as he maneuvers his wheelchair with sheer precision through the obstacle of dumbbells and weight machines. He stops and analyzes individuals as they work out, sometimes commenting, and other times analyzing with meticulous accuracy, whether the desired outcome is being achieved. He frequently refers to the notes he makes in his electronic notebook. Kyle understands the importance of syncing mind, body and spirit, and inspires athletes in their journey to reach that premiere number, 10. He understands, at a level few of us can, that we are more than just the sum of our body parts. Kyle is disciplined, and goofing off will be rewarded with an intensified work-out. The lesson: Kids come back for more rather than quit. His impact is immeasurable. Kyle has more to offer young people physically, mentally and spiritually, than any other person I know. The key is to listen and act on his words. God indeed had a plan. If anyone can personify the results of a synced mind, body and spirit it is Kyle Francis.

> *You have meaningful work to do,*
> *and a beautiful vision to express,*
> *and today is your opportunity to do it.*
> —PHIL WEBB, CONSULTANT

I remember one particular track and field meet against a rival school. We were the visiting team and the competition was intense. Kyle gave the pre-game pep talk, and in it he described the five things in life that were most important to him:

1 His military uniform and its tattered remains hanging
   on his wall.

2 His family. Yes, his biological family but also his Marine
   family and those people that he really, truly knows—
   authentic relationships.

3 Me, which I didn't expect to hear.

4 His crucifix, which hangs in a prominent spot in his apartment.

5 A mirror. He awakes each morning and looks in the mirror
   to welcome a new day, a self-determined sunrise ritual that
   motivates him to continue.

The track meet was close through every event and it came down to the
last race. Our team came out victorious. A few days later I ran into the
opposing team's coach, and he told me that after that meet he sat in his
driveway for half an hour wondering how he let the win escape his grasp.
I said one word: "Kyle." His words make young people believe in themselves, and what they can attain, at a level others just can't convey.

Kyle is also a member of the coaching staff at Christian Brothers Academy
(CBA), a local powerhouse football team. He assists with summer strength
and conditioning sessions and handles junior varsity defensive coordi-
nator duties. Casey Brown, head coach of the football program, describes
Kyle in these words. "The addition of Kyle Francis to the CBA football staff
is perfect on so many different and unique levels. This young man is an
inspiration to the staff, our athletes and the CBA community as a whole.
As a US Marine veteran, who was wounded in Afghanistan, he can share
detailed real-life accounts of commitment, sacrifice, and brotherhood. As
a person living with ALS, Kyle shows us all what he can do, all of the time.
You're tired? You're having a bad day? Things didn't go your way today?

Sure we all have those days and those thoughts, but one look at Kyle and your perspective on life and what you can't do changes quickly."

Brown goes on to say, "A person like Kyle reminds us that we are blessed, and we can motivate ourselves in a positive direction, physically, emotionally, and spiritually. We are the only ones stopping our goals. Sure, adjustments need to be made along our timeline of life, but our individual ultimate goal still exists. I truly believe that certain people come into our lives for reasons unknown to us. I am a better person today because of Kyle's work and inspiration within the CBA family."

In the movie, "The Equalizer," an action thriller movie adapted from the 1980s TV series of the same name, Denzel Washington plays the role of retired special forces operative, Robert McCall. McCall comes out of his quiet retirement working at a home improvement megastore to serve retribution against anyone who would brutalize the helpless. Mark Twain's quote about finding your life's purpose, (see page 88), scrolls at the beginning of the movie. McCall puts three principles above all else: body, mind and soul. When a young woman tells McCall life is tough, he tells her to "change your world." As an action thriller, the movie has clear violence as part of the theme, but the lead character's message is quite introspective.

In a different context, but with the same pensive message, Kyle, too, has chosen to change his world. He has chosen to be a survivor rather than a victim, to work with me in developing the mind, body and spirit of aspiring young athletes. He remains driven, determined and has a soul purpose. Against great odds, he continues to achieve. Kyle is a 10 in my book. When so many people would pity themselves, and question God's purpose, Kyle begins each day prepared to seek out opportunity. Kyle accepts and faithfully believes he has found the answer to "Why?"

CHAPTER EIGHT

I am
me

I'VE BEEN COACHING high school girls' indoor and outdoor track and field for many years now. The school stadium that houses our track and field is a great facility for both practice, and hosting events throughout the season. But prior to those warmer temperatures, the indoor team must resign themselves to the typically cold and snowy winter that is routine for the Central New York area. There is little, if any, opportunity to train outside, and space is at a premium for the various teams training indoors. My team congregates to begin practice every day in a small space in the lower back hallway. By incorporating rotations in the weight room and supplemental circuit training, we make it work. And as I've said before, a good coach can train an athlete anywhere. I've been blessed with teams that regularly win league and sectional titles, and frequently have athletes that qualify for events at the state championship level. But, in the last few years, I've been blessed with a much different kind of a win as well. It's a win that nurtures my soul, and enriches my spirit.

It started with a teen named Meghan, a junior at the time, who was interested in joining the track team. She had never before participated on a school sports team, but loved to run. The indoor track team seemed like a good fit. When she approached me and asked if she could compete, I said, "Yes." For the first several practices, Meghan was a bit overwhelmed with the expectations. She soon found out there would be no personalized favors or special treatment. Meghan needed to learn the practice routines, get the sequences and procedures down, and work. Work hard. Her other teammates assisted Meghan as they could, but it would ultimately be up to her to do what needed to be done. Meghan struggled, but persevered. Weeks of practice passed and then the day she'd envisioned finally arrived.

Meghan would run the 4x2 (each of four runners complete 200-meters) with three other girls on the team. The competition was held at a local community college arena. Meghan was a bundle of excitement and nerves as she looked into the crowd at her family, proudly positioned in the stands, ready to cheer her on. The race began. Meghan was positioned as the anchor leg, or the last runner, of the relay team. As the baton was passed to her, the entire crowd began to cheer and Meghan began to run as she had never run before. As Meghan crossed the finish line, the crowd erupted into applause. Was it because her relay team had just won the race? In regard to the fastest time, no. But in spirit, they had won the hearts of everyone there. Meghan had just demonstrated to an arena full of people how a teen, who happens to have Down syndrome, can run the "dis" out of disability.

Meghan went on to finish the indoor season, and competed on that school year's spring track and field team as well. She competed in the 100-, 200- and 800-meter, along with the shot put. As the fall semester of the following school year settled in and the next indoor track season approached, three more of Meghan's friends, including teen girls, Gabby and Thea, decided to join the team. Each of the girls has what would typically be classified as a disability. Fortunately they all classify themselves quite differently.

The friends would compete in separate events and then join together for their own identifiable, yet delightfully ordinary, relay team. They ran the 4x2 relay alongside other schools competing at each meet. It was truly a win-win situation for everyone involved.

This year, the girls are ready for the outdoor track and field season. They've developed into confident members of our team, our family. Social interactions often happen best spontaneously, so I have let those moments of connection among the athletes happen naturally. We all learn from each other and respect one another. All of the athletes on the team treat each other as they would want to be treated. They have each learned valuable life lessons about respect and the appreciation of what another person may have to offer—if you just get to know them. Athletically, we train hard as a team but the lesson is not always about attaining physical excellence. A winner in life should have a diversified mind and inclusive spirit as well.

Many reading this chapter may be thinking about the opportunity Special Olympics has to offer and the notion that it would seem to be a safer, more appropriate, option. After all, Special Olympics were created for athletes that have an intellectual disability. Gabby has been involved in both. Her mom, Cheri, responds in this way:

"When asked what the difference is for my daughter, Gabby, to participate in Special Olympic sports and school sports, the answer is sometimes hard for people to understand. Until you have a child that is physically a little weaker and slower athletically than the "average" individual, it is hard to put into perspective. I can only tell you what the differences have meant to me, as Gabby's mom. When Gabby was little, my husband and I got her involved her in youth sports. The coaches were very welcoming and tried to work with her but the reality of the situation, no matter how safe the coaches tried to be, was that—compared to her teammates—Gabby was at a greater risk of getting injured. Her balance was underdeveloped, and she really could not keep up. As a parent it was hard to watch. When physical danger became apparent, we looked for another way for our young daughter to stay active. It was at this time, our relationship with Special Olympics began. For us, this was a way for Gabby to play contact sports, and remain safe. Years later, she continues to compete with others who share similar abilities. She found friends in those early years that have developed into long-lasting relationships. To me, there's more to Special Olympics than the physical aspect of playing a sport. Special Olympics creates a community that envelops individuals with unconditional love. The sport is as much about learning as it is staying healthy and doing the best you can. Participation has also given Gabby a chance to travel with a team for overnight stays that help foster her independence. Gabby may never make it to a state championship on a high school team, but she has advanced to state-level competitions for Special Olympics on several occasions. Gabby has learned, and lived, the motto of Special Olympics: 'Let me win, but if I cannot win, let me be brave in the attempt.' "

Cheri's response continues with a fast forward to Gabby's senior year in high school. "After watching a friend of Gabby's have success the previous year, while participating on the school's track team, Gabby decided to give it a try. There is something to be said for being a part of an athletic team when you are in high school. You can walk down the hall and others will say *hello*. They cheer for you and care for you, on and off the athletic field. You travel to other locations for events, ride the bus with your peers and get to be around others that are the same age as you."

> *Every student wants to be a part of their school*
> *community. And that is what track and field*
> *has done for Gabby.*
> —CHERI, GABBY'S MOM

"She sees other teammates out in the community, and they say *hello* to her. She is excited to see them and, as a mom, it is really neat to see. Gabby has an extra bounce in her step, and she is always excited to go to school and participate in track practice. Being a member of the track team has truly been inspirational. When you watch Coach Pete with the kids, you see him treat them all as equals. I remember arriving at practice one day to pick the kids up, and he was telling the students that he was going to simulate what the upcoming track event would be like for some of the teammates that have not run, so that they would be prepared. He never referred to them as different or needing special assistance, just teammates that have not done this before. It brought tears to my eyes as the entire team sat and cheered for a relay team that had never participated in a track event before. Today, as I retell this event, tears still roll down my cheeks."

Cheri concludes by stating, "That unconditional support and openness to accept and to encourage all students to be all they can be is what my daughter, Gabby, being on this track team, has meant to me. It means more than any words could ever express. So remember, if you are ever given the opportunity to open your arms, or include someone who is differently abled, you are not only teaching them, but you are teaching every student involved what it means to accept all of us for our individual differences."

When Gabby was asked by her mom what she thinks about being on the track team she commented with a smile, "Coach Moore is my favorite coach because he thinks I am his perfect athlete. My teammates cheer each other on. We make new friends and have fun."

Her fellow teammate, Thea, puts it into these words: "What I enjoy about being on the girls' track team at my high school is running. I love to run fast! I like making new friends and we support each other. They clap and yell my name to cheer me on, and I cheer for them too. Coach Pete helps me learn the form to run fast. 'Pick up those knees,' he tells me. Just because I have Down syndrome doesn't mean I can't run. I am so happy for Coach Pete because he is happy to have me on the team, and I am happy, too."

Meghan adds, "I like to run with my friends, Liz and Nicole."

Liz, a sophomore on the track team, says this about the makeup of their wonderfully diverse track team: "These girls put a smile on my face every time I see them. Many people don't think that individuals with disabilities are capable of doing what "normal people" can do. These people are wrong. Thea, Meghan and Gabby work hard every day at school and at track. They are a blessing in my life, and I am proud to call them my friends."

> *The only disability in life is a bad attitude.*
> —SCOTT HAMILTON, RETIRED AMERICAN
> FIGURE SKATER AND OLYMPIC MEDALIST

It is natural to want to fit in, to be socially accepted, to be "normal." Often the ability to be acknowledged or recognized for who you are is hampered by judgment, a lack of understanding, narrow-mindedness or assumptions.

> *The first step toward change is awareness.*
> *The second step is acceptance."*
> —NATHANIEL BRANDEN, PSYCHOTHERAPIST

There is a quote from an unknown author that reads: "Don't judge me until you know me. Don't underestimate me until you challenge me, and don't talk about me until you've talked to me."

How true.

So what IS normal? The meaning of the word *(dis)ability*, as well as the word *normal*, is often a matter of opinion. Perception. What is perceived as a typical, or average, performance or level of normality for one person, may be completely different for another. An athlete exhibiting a superior level of athleticism can clearly benefit a team in any sport, but the most unlikely athlete can, possibly, have an unimaginable impact on a team's inspiration and motivation. Those individuals who may be perceived as "outside of the norm," may naturally hold the core of what other athletes strive for: spirit, drive, determination and purpose. It's not about having a disability, but having a different ability.

Robert Hensel, a 46-year-old athlete and straight-talking advocate, born with spina bifida, sends this message out to the world: "Know me for my abilities, not my disability." He, too, chooses not to put "dis" in his ability. Hensel is the Guinness World Record holder for the longest non-stop wheelie in a wheelchair, a distance of 6.178 miles.

The mother of a son with Down syndrome has a wonderful picture of her teen posted on her website, myquestforhealing.com, following a basketball game. He only played a few minutes and their team lost the game, but on that day, it wasn't about the score. A quote at the bottom of the page reads "Winning is in the eye of the beholder." Sometimes the winning score is not the winning moment of a game. Fortunately, there have been many stories about athletic competitions that place inspiration, encouragement and the chance-of-a-lifetime before the big win. In some cases, the big win comes as a bonus. Each story has the same humbling message of opportunity.

I have high expectations for all of the athletes on my track team. Do I have a faster relay team than Gabby, Thea, Meghan and their other teammate? Yes. Do I have a more determined relay team? No. If you have trained your hardest, tried your best and, in this case, run your fastest, you have won. On this team, as with all the teams I coach, we are a family. We all support each other, we learn from each other and we care for one another.

There is an old Indian tale, author unknown, which reads as follows:

> *One evening an old Cherokee told his grandson about a battle that goes on inside people. He said, "My son, the battle is between two "wolves" inside us all.*
>
> *One is Evil. It is anger, envy, jealousy, sorrow, regret, greed, arrogance, self-pity, guilt, resentment, inferiority, lies, false pride, superiority, and ego.*
>
> *The other is Good. It is joy, peace, love, hope, serenity, humility, kindness, benevolence, empathy, generosity, truth, compassion, and faith."*
>
> *The grandson thought about it for a minute and then asked his grandfather: "Which wolf wins?"*
>
> *The old Cherokee simply replied, "The one you feed."*

So which wolf will you feed? Which emotion or attitude will dictate who you are, whether on the athletic field, or off? As a teammate, a coach, a spectator, friend or stranger, will your positivity have a full belly, or will negativity fill your plate?

Maya Angelou writes: "I've learned that people will forget what you said, people will forget what you did, but people will never forget how you made them feel."

Sync your mind, sync your body, and sync your spirit. Aspire. Believe. Work Hard. And Achieve.

CHAPTER NINE

Dream big

PEOPLE SAY I BRING SUCCESS. I'm not sure if that qualifies as perception or reality, but every time I hear those words, I silently thank God. The success referred to may be an individual's personal triumph or a team accomplishment, a short-term goal or a milestone achievement. It doesn't matter. My prayers are always steadfast, proclaimed with gratitude from my heart. What I can tell you is that I am confident about where God has placed me in my journey. I have synced my own mind, body and spirit, and I believe that wherever I go, I will succeed. And though that statement may seem arrogant, it truly isn't. I am a humble man. That mindset is simply my motivation, my purpose. A purpose I believe. And one you can believe in as well.

> *Think twice before you speak, because your*
> *words and influence will plant the seed of either*
> *success or failure in the mind of another.*
> —*NAPOLEON HILL, AMERICAN AUTHOR*

I have found that when working with young athletes, you are always talking to someone—the players, the parents, a colleague, a coach—the list goes on, and on. I have also come to realize that there are many day-to-day opportunities for any one of us to react to these conversations in a positive, or negative, manner. That decision is ours to make, and ours alone. The context of a conversation can be an event, a person, or possibly a circumstance. Regardless, we must live with our response or reaction. When deciding an outcome, or the desired effect of a conversation, I always try to remember a common rule of engagement: Think before you speak, or act. I will often pause, if even for the briefest moment, before responding or reacting and ask myself, "What would God do?" or more specifically, "What would God want me to do?" Those few moments of reflective pause can often give a person the opportunity to transform an outcome. The Lord's thoughts and ways are his own, and I am not suggesting we try to act as God. I am suggesting we conduct ourselves with Christ-like character, or behaviors representative of his purpose. Choosing to take that pause can have long-term significance. It can be the difference between being seen as a person of good moral character, or an individual viewed as disrespectable or belligerent.

> *Your word is a lamp to my feet*
> *and a light to my path.*
> —PSALMS *119:105*

There are two common phrases that seem to seep into my thoughts on a regular basis. They are inspirational sayings that offer wonderful basic advice. The first is an old cliché that has been rewritten in a variety of ways. My favorite version reads: "Always look to where you are going, not at where you have been." The second saying, "Don't listen to what people say, watch what they do," has also been revised over the years. A simpler version circles back to what my mother impressed upon me at an early age. As I wrote in the introduction of this book, she would say, "Watch and listen. Always watch and listen."

I often go to the mall with my wife and, as she shops, I just walk. I'm a black guy with a tie-dyed T-shirt, strolling along, occasionally stopping for a rest by a storefront, or on a bench in the concourse area. As I maneuver my way around the crowds of people, I am always amazed at the number of kids who will just stop and start a conversation with me. My parents have always said that I am a Pied Piper, of sorts, very approachable. But I also welcome the idea of approachability, and willingly acknowledge that my demeanor invites conversation. Whether I am at a mall, at work, at church, coaching, training or wherever, I attract people. I use this God-given gift to reach out to others, as well. There are two very easy acts of kindness I try to follow through on every day, and so can you. The first is effortless: When you pass by someone, particularly if they have their head down, say "Hello." That's it, say "Hello." It's a small, simple word that packs a lot of power. Now I know it may not seem feasible on a busy city sidewalk, or a crowded corridor, but at least try. A few friendly gestures are better than none at all. I also suggest that you try to meet a new person every day. Because much of my work involves youth, I often try to seek out a young person who seems like they could use a friendly introduction.

In this book I outline my belief in inspiring young athletes to sync their mind, body and spirit. Inspiration can be defined as the ability to stimulate, excite or motivate. But the word *inspired* has biblical roots as well. It is a translation of the Greek word *theopneustos*, meaning God-breathed, or, to arouse one's true abilities through divine influence. I want to inspire and faithfully challenge young people to reach new heights.

> *Cogito, ergo sum,*
> —RENÉ DESCARTES, FRENCH MATHEMATICIAN,
> SCIENTIST, AND PHILOSOPHER

At one time or another we have all heard the phrase: "I think, therefore I am." These words, from the well-known Latin translation, originated with the famous French philosopher and mathematician, René Descartes, also known as the Father of Modern Philosophy. This celebrated expression has been converted into sports mantras like, "I ski, therefore I am," as well as popular slogans that identify other special interests.

Much of Descartes' philosophical thinking led him to speculate about the connection between the mind and the body. The concept—if we know we are thinking, we know we exist—is the focus of this quote. Though debatable among some scholars, Descartes was a very faithful man and hoped his philosophical evidence would defend the Christian faith, and the existence of God.

My ability to inspire young people to sync their mind, body and spirit in the present, is drawn from concepts presented to our culture centuries ago. In formulating one's personal motivators, perhaps a Descartes-based mantra could be "I have purpose, therefore I am."

Listed below are a few of the many words of gratitude I have received over time. I have chosen to include a few of these email and text messages as a reflection of what other young athletes can become, and as expressions of true appreciation. All kids dream. All kids aspire. All kids wish and hope. All kids have potential, promise and the possibility for great things to occur.

- "Thank you for not giving up on me"
  —*Jasmine Thompson (East Carolina Track and Field)*

- "Without your help, our daughter's dream of playing college basketball could not have been possible."
  —*Craig Norris (father of Emily who plays basketball for Mercyhurst College).*

- "Thank you for giving me the insight I needed. Trust God and stay focused."
  —*Megan Salle (ESPN intern)*

- "Pete, you saved my son's life. You gave my son a new life. You gave my son hope and courage. Pete, your belief in my son made him believe in himself. You will always be my son's guardian angel."
  —*Olivia Bennigan (parent of Christian Brothers Academy football player).*

- "U truly have been a blessing for me and my program. When I think of how much u have done for me, it brings tears to my eyes. Thanks so much, Pete."
  —*Anthony Talarico (Bishop Grimes head football coach. The team played in the 2014 high school national football federation league championship game. It was the first title finals for the school in 33 years).*

- "Thanks for believing in us when nobody else did."
  —*Joe Hakizimana (Bishop Grimes football player awarded MVP at 2014 championship game)*

- "You're amazing. I've been so lucky to learn from you."
  —*Alicia Sherlock (College of St. Rose)*

- "I just want to say thank you for all the chances you give, the things you preach and lessons I've learned from you. It's been a blessing."
  —*Tori Cipoli (high school track and field)*

- "You never fail to amaze me."
  —*Chelsea Davidson (former high school athlete)*

- "You just don't understand how much I appreciate what you do for me and for everyone."

  —*Luke D. (high school baseball player)*

> *God's gift to us: Potential.*
> *Our gift to God: Developing it.*
> —ROBERT J. FASHANO,
> CEO ALLIANCE ADVISORY GROUP

If you're a coach, or a family member reading this book, give a young person your time, your interest, your experience, your attention. If you're a young person reading this book, seek out your desire, your motivation and your purpose in whatever it is you are trying to achieve. For everyone reading this book, have faith.

> *I've said it all along that God is in control.*
> —TONY DUNGY, AUTHOR,
> FORMER PROFESSIONAL FOOTBALL PLAYER
> AND NFL COACH

As a not-so-young man anymore, my long-term plan seems to be getting shorter, but I have a dream, just as the young athletes I work with have. My dream is to someday be swinging in a hammock, on a white sandy beach, with my dread locks and a long beard. Will it ever happen? Who knows, but the idea does put a smile on my face. What I do know is that my future is in God's hands, and he already has a plan for me, and for you, too. And I'm okay with that!

ACKNOWLEDGMENTS

FROM PETE

To Renee and Ray: I owe you everything.

To God for shining his light on me.

To Pat Kennedy and his family:
    Thanks for your true friendship.

To Pastor Andre Dowdell and his family:
    I can't thank you enough for all
    your prayers and friendship.

To my mother and father, and 'big sis,' Yolanda:
    Thanks for all your unconditional love.

To my wife, Theresa, who loves and believes in me.

To my son, Bryce: I am so proud to be your dad.

To all who have helped me along this journey: Thank you.

FROM RENEE

To my longtime friend, Nancy:
    Thank you for your commitment to this project.
    You're the best!

To Claire: Thank you for your expertise in editing.

To my husband, Ray: Your love and support is cherished.

To Pete, my good friend: Our paths were meant to cross.

REFERENCES

D'Annunzio, Steve. *The Prosperity Paradigm*. Hewlett, NY: White Light Press, 2006.

Descartes, René. *Meditations on First Philosophy 1644*. (Principles of Philosophy), Part 1, article 7.

Ditota, Donna. "Breanna Stewart on verge of becoming best women's basketball player in world, experts say." (http://blog.syracuse.com/sports/print.html?entry=/2014/08/could_breanna_stewart_become_the_best_womens_basketball_player_of_all_time.html). Syracuse.com, 2014-08-06. Retrieved 2014-08-06.

Forbis, Jim. *Is Your Future Bigger Than Your Past?* Toronto, Canada: MDRT.org, 2014.

Horn, T.S. *Advances in Sport Psychology.* Champaign, IL: Human Kinetics, 2008.

Macrae, Fiona. "Why classical music can inspire you to exercise: Relaxing qualities can reduce heart rate and blood pressure." Science Correspondent: Daily Mail.com, 2013-1-20. Retrieved 2014-10-13.

Martin, Ralph. *The Fulfillment of All Desire.* Steubenville, OH: Emmaus Road Publishing, 2006.

Moyo, Max. *The 8th Wonder of the World.* Toronto, Canada: MDRT.org, 2013.

Nevid, Jeffrey. *Psychology: Concepts and Applications.* Boston, MA: Houghton Mifflin Company, 2009.

NFL website. "NFL Events: Draft Player Profiles—Tyvon Branch." (http://www.nfl.com/draft/2011/profiles/tyvon- branch?id=1681) nfldraft.com, 2011. Retrieved 2014-12-18.

Peale, Norman Vincent. *The Power of Positive Thinking.* New York, NY: Simon & Schuster, 2008.

Phipps, Wintley. *Moments of Destiny.* Toronto, Canada: MDRT.org, 2013.

Pink, Daniel. *Drive: The Surprising Truth About What Motivates Us.* New York, NY: Riverhead Books, 2009.

Ruden, Dave. "New BBCOR bats simulate wooden bats, force hitters to have better mechanics." Stamfordadvocate.com, 2012-3-31. Retrieved 2014-8-19.

The Quote Garden (www.quotegarden.com/attitude.html) quotegarden. com. 2014-11-06. Retrieved 2014-11-23.

The Quote Garden (www.quotegarden.com/adversity.html) quotegarden.com. 2014-08-16. Retrieved 2014-11-24.

Wikipedia. "Tyvon Branch" (http://en.wikipedia.org/wiki/Tyvon_Branch) *Wikipedia.com.* 2014-12-18. Retrieved 2014-12-18.

Warren, Rick. *The Purpose Driven Life.* Grand Rapids, Michigan: Zondervan, 2002.

Webb, Donnie. "Dying mom's premonition came true, Mitch Dunay of C-NS will play football at Princeton." (http://highschoolsports. syracuse.com/news/article/5740415834253192801 /moms-awesome). Syacuse.com. 2014-4-03. Retrieved 2014-12-01.